NEW &
COLLECTED
POEMS
1952–1992

POETRY BY GEOFFREY HILL

For the Unfallen

King Log

Mercian Hymns

Somewhere Is Such a Kingdom:
Poems, 1952–1971

Tenebrae

The Mystery of the Charity of Charles Péguy

New and Collected Poems, 1952–1992

Geoffrey Hill

NEW &
COLLECTED
POEMS
1952–1992

Houghton Mifflin Company

BOSTON   NEW YORK

1994

For information about permission to reproduce
selections from this book, write to Permissions,
Houghton Mifflin Company, 215 Park Avenue South,
New York, New York 10003.

Library of Congress Cataloging-in-Publication Data
Hill, Geoffrey.
New and collected poems, 1952–1992 / Geoffrey Hill.
p.   cm.
ISBN 0-395-68087-5(cl) ISBN 0-395-68086-7 (pbk)
I. Title.
PR6015.14735N48   1994   93-5010
821'.914 — dc20   CIP

Printed in the United States of America

AGM 10 9 8 7 6 5 4 3 2 1

to Donald Hall

Contents

FOR THE UNFALLEN (1959)

Genesis   *3*
God's Little Mountain   *6*
Holy Thursday   *7*
Merlin   *8*
The Bidden Guest   *9*
In Memory of Jane Fraser   *11*
The Turtle Dove   *12*
The Troublesome Reign   *13*
Solomon's Mines   *14*
The Distant Fury of Battle   *15*
Asmodeus   *16*
Requiem for the Plantagenet Kings   *18*
Two Formal Elegies   *19*
Metamorphoses   *21*
Picture of a Nativity   *26*
Canticle for Good Friday   *27*
The Guardians   *28*
The White Ship   *29*
Wreaths   *30*
Elegiac Stanzas   *31*
After Cumae   *32*
Little Apocalypse   *33*
The Bibliographers   *34*
Of Commerce and Society   *35*
Doctor Faustus   *41*
A Pastoral   *43*
Orpheus and Eurydice   *44*
In Piam Memoriam   *45*
To the (Supposed) Patron   *46*

KING LOG (1968)

Ovid in the Third Reich   *49*
Annunciations   *50*
Locust Songs   *52*
I Had Hope When Violence Was Ceas't   *54*
September Song   *55*
An Order of Service   *56*
The Humanist   *57*
Funeral Music   *58*
Four Poems Regarding the Endurance of Poets   *66*
The Imaginative Life   *70*
The Assisi Fragments   *71*
History as Poetry   *72*
Soliloquies   *73*
Cowan Bridge   *75*
Fantasia on 'Horbury'   *76*
Three Baroque Meditations   *77*
The Songbook of Sebastian Arrurruz   *80*

MERCIAN HYMNS (1971)

I   The Naming of Offa   *93*
II   The Naming of Offa   *94*
III   The Crowning of Offa   *95*
IV   The Crowning of Offa   *96*
V   The Crowning of Offa   *97*
VI   The Childhood of Offa   *98*
VII   The Kingdom of Offa   *99*
VIII   Offa's Leechdom   *100*
IX   Offa's Book of the Dead   *101*
X   Offa's Laws   *102*
XI   Offa's Coins   *103*
XII   Offa's Coins   *104*
XIII   Offa's Coins   *105*
XIV   Offa's Laws   *106*
XV   Offa's Bestiary   *107*

XVI	Offa's Sword	*108*
XVII	Offa's Journey to Rome	*109*
XVIII	Offa's Journey to Rome	*110*
XIX	Offa's Laws	*111*
XX	Offa's 'Defence of the English People'	*112*
XXI	The Kingdom of Offa	*113*
XXII	Offa's 'Second Defence of the English People'	*114*
XXIII	Opus Anglicanum	*115*
XXIV	Opus Anglicanum	*116*
XXV	Opus Anglicanum	*117*
XXVI	Offa's Bestiary	*118*
XXVII	The Death of Offa	*119*
XXVIII	The Death of Offa	*120*
XXIX	The Death of Offa	*121*
XXX	The Death of Offa	*122*

TENEBRAE (1978)

The Pentecost Castle   *125*
Lachrimae   *133*
An Apology for the Revival of Christian
       Architecture In England   *140*
Two Chorale-Preludes   *153*
A Pre-Raphaelite Notebook   *155*
Terribilis Est Locus Iste   *156*
Veni Coronaberis   *157*
Florentines   *158*
'Christmas Trees'   *159*
Tenebrae   *160*

THE MYSTERY OF THE CHARITY
OF CHARLES PÉGUY (1983)   *163*

Hymns to Our Lady of Chartres   *180*

NEW POEMS (1992)

Sobieski's Shield   *185*
Of Coming-into-Being and Passing-Away   *186*
Ritornelli   *187*
Canaan   *188*
Respublica   *190*
Song Contest   *191*
De Jure Belli ac Pacis   *192*
Scenes with Harlequins   *194*
To the Nieuport Scout   *201*
Churchill's Funeral   *202*
Psalms of Assize   *209*
Cycle   *211*
Sorrel   *213*

NOTES AND ACKNOWLEDGEMENTS   *215*

INDEX OF TITLES AND FIRST LINES   *221*

FOR THE UNFALLEN

Genesis

I

Against the burly air I strode
Crying the miracles of God.

And first I brought the sea to bear
Upon the dead weight of the land;
And the waves flourished at my prayer,
The rivers spawned their sand.

And where the streams were salt and full
The tough pig-headed salmon strove,
Ramming the ebb, in the tide's pull,
To reach the steady hills above.

II

The second day I stood and saw
The osprey plunge with triggered claw,
Feathering blood along the shore,
To lay the living sinew bare.

And the third day I cried: 'Beware
The soft-voiced owl, the ferret's smile,
The hawk's deliberate stoop in air,
Cold eyes, and bodies hooped in steel,
Forever bent upon the kill.'

III

And I renounced, on the fourth day,
This fierce and unregenerate clay,

Building as a huge myth for man
The watery Leviathan,

And made the long-winged albatross
Scour the ashes of the sea
Where Capricorn and Zero cross,
A brooding immortality —
Such as the charmed phoenix has
In the unwithering tree.

IV

The phoenix burns as cold as frost;
And, like a legendary ghost,
The phantom-bird goes wild and lost,
Upon a pointless ocean tossed.

So, the fifth day, I turned again
To flesh and blood and the blood's pain.

V

On the sixth day, as I rode
In haste about the works of God,
With spurs I plucked the horse's blood.

By blood we live, the hot, the cold,
To ravage and redeem the world:
There is no bloodless myth will hold.

And by Christ's blood are men made free
Though in close shrouds their bodies lie
Under the rough pelt of the sea;

Though Earth has rolled beneath her weight
The bones that cannot bear the light.

God's Little Mountain

Below, the river scrambled like a goat
Dislodging stones. The mountain stamped its foot,
Shaking, as from a trance. And I was shut
With wads of sound into a sudden quiet.

I thought the thunder had unsettled heaven,
All was so still. And yet the sky was riven
By flame that left the air cold and engraven.
I waited for the word that was not given,

Pent up into a region of pure force,
Made subject to the pressure of the stars;
I saw the angels lifted like pale straws;
I could not stand before those winnowing eyes

And fell, until I found the world again.
Now I lack grace to tell what I have seen;
For though the head frames words the tongue has none.
And who will prove the surgeon to this stone?

Holy Thursday

Naked, he climbed to the wolf's lair;
He beheld Eden without fear,
Finding no ambush offered there
But sleep under the harbouring fur.

He said: 'They are decoyed by love
Who, tarrying through the hollow grove,
Neglect the seasons' sad remove.
Child and nurse walk hand in glove

As unaware of Time's betrayal,
Weaving their innocence with guile.
But they must cleave the fire's peril
And suffer innocence to fall.

I have been touched with that fire,
And have fronted the she-wolf's lair.
Lo, she lies gentle and innocent of desire
Who was my constant myth and terror.'

Merlin

I will consider the outnumbering dead:
For they are the husks of what was rich seed.
Now, should they come together to be fed,
They would outstrip the locusts' covering tide.

Arthur, Elaine, Mordred; they are all gone
Among the raftered galleries of bone.
By the long barrows of Logres they are made one,
And over their city stands the pinnacled corn.

The Bidden Guest

The starched unbending candles stir
As though a wind had caught their hair,
As though the surging of a host
Had charged the air of Pentecost.
And I believe in the spurred flame,
Those racing tongues, but cannot come
Out of my heart's unbroken room;
Nor feel the lips of fire among
The cold light and the chilling song,
The broken mouths that spill their hoard
Of prayer like beads on to a board.
There, at the rail, each muffled head
Swings sombrely. O quiet deed.
This is the breaking of the bread;
On this the leanest heart may feed
When by the stiffly-linened priest
All wounds of light are newly dressed,
Healed by the pouring-in of wine
From bitter as from sweet grapes bled.
But one man lay beneath his vine
And, waking, found that it was dead.
And so my heart has ceased to breathe
(Though there God's worm blunted its head
And stayed.) And still I seem to smile.
Wounds have thick lips and cannot tell
If there is blackness couched beneath.
'Yet there are wounds, unquenched with oil,
And blazing eyes that would compel
Evil to turn, though like a mole
It dug blind alleys down the soil.'
So I heard once. But now I hear,

Like shifted blows at my numb back,
A grinding heel; a scraped chair.
The heart's tough shell is still to crack
When, spent of all its wine and bread,
Unwinkingly the altar lies
Wreathed in its sour breath, cold and dead.
A server has put out its eyes.

In Memory of Jane Fraser

When snow like sheep lay in the fold
And winds went begging at each door,
And the far hills were blue with cold,
And a cold shroud lay on the moor,

She kept the siege. And every day
We watched her brooding over death
Like a strong bird above its prey.
The room filled with the kettle's breath.

Damp curtains glued against the pane
Sealed time away. Her body froze
As if to freeze us all, and chain
Creation to a stunned repose.

She died before the world could stir.
In March the ice unloosed the brook
And water ruffled the sun's hair.
Dead cones upon the alder shook.

The Turtle Dove

Love that drained her drained him she'd loved, though each
For the other's sake forged passion upon speech,
Bore their close days through sufferance towards night
Where she at length grasped sleep and he lay quiet

As though needing no questions, now, to guess
What her secreting heart could not well hide.
Her caught face flinched in half-sleep at his side.
Yet she, by day, modelled her real distress,

Poised, turned her cheek to the attending world
Of children and intriguers and the old;
Conversed freely, exercised, was admired,
Being strong to dazzle. All this she endured

To affront him. He watched her rough grief work
Under the formed surface of habit. She spoke
Like one long undeceived but she was hurt.
She denied more love, yet her starved eyes caught

His, devouring, at times. Then, as one self-dared,
She went to him, plied there; like a furious dove
Bore down with visitations of such love
As his lithe, fathoming heart absorbed and buried.

The Troublesome Reign

So much he had from fashion and no more:
Her trained hard gaze, brief lips whose laughter spat
Concession to desire. She suffered that,
Feeding a certain green-fuel to his fire.

Reluctant heat! This burning of the dead
Could consume her also. She moved apart
As if, through such denial, he might be made
Himself again familiar and unscarred,

Contained, even wary, though not too much
To take pleasure considering her flesh shone,
Her salt-worn summer dress. But he had gone
Thirty days through such a dream of taste and touch

When the sun stood for him and the violent larks
Stabbed up into the sun. She was his, then;
Her limbs grasped him, satisfied, while his brain
Judged every move and cry from its separate dark.

More dark, more separate, now, yet still not dead,
Their mouths being drawn to public and private speech —
Though there was too much care in all he said,
A hard kind of no-feeling in her touch —

By such rites they saved love's face, and such laws
As prescribe mutual tolerance, charity
To neighbours, strangers, those by nature
Subdued among famines and difficult wars.

Solomon's Mines

To Bonamy Dobrée

Anything to have done!
(The eagle flagged to the sun)
To have discovered and disclosed
The buried thrones, the means used;

Spadework and symbol; each deed
Resurrecting those best dead
Priests, soldiers and kings;
Blazed-out, stripped-out things;

Anything to get up and go
(Let the hewn gates clash to)
Without looking round
Out of that strong land.

The Distant Fury of Battle

Grass resurrects to mask, to strangle,
Words glossed on stone, lopped stone-angel;
But the dead maintain their ground —
That there's no getting round —

Who in places vitally rest,
Named, anonymous; who test
Alike the endurance of yews
Laurels, moonshine, stone, all tissues;

With whom, under licence and duress,
There are pacts made, if not peace.
Union with the stone-wearing dead
Claims the born leader, the prepared

Leader, the devourers and all lean men.
Some, finally, learn to begin.
Some keep to the arrangement of love
(Or similar trust) under whose auspices move

Most subjects, toward the profits of this
Combine of doves and witnesses.
Some, dug out of hot-beds, are brought bare,
Not past conceiving but past care.

Asmodeus

They, after the slow building of the house,
Furnished it; brought warmth under the skin.
Tiles, that a year's rough wind could rattle loose,
Being close-pressed still kept storms out and storms in.
(Of all primed and vain citadels, to choose
This, to choose this of all times to begin!)
Acknowledging, they said, one who pursues
Hobbies of serious lust and indoor sin,
Clearly they both stood, lovers without fear,
Might toy with fire brought dangerously to hand
To tame, not exorcize, spirits; though the air
Whistled abstracted menace, could confound
Strength by device, by music reaching the ear,
Lightning conducted forcibly to the ground.

2

The night, then; bravely stiffen; you are one
Whom stars could burn more deeply than the sun,
Guide-book martyr. You, doubtless, hear wings,
Too sheer for cover, swift; the scattered noise
Of darkness looming with propitious things;
And nests of rumour clustered in the world.
So drummed, so shadowed, your mere trudging voice
Might rave at large while easy truths were told,
Bad perjurable stuff, to be forgiven
Because of this lame journey out of mind.
A tax on men to seventy-times-seven,
A busy vigilance of goose and hound,
Keeps up all guards. Since you are outside, go,
Closing the doors of the house and the head also.

Requiem for the Plantagenet Kings

For whom the possessed sea littered, on both shores,
Ruinous arms; being fired, and for good,
To sound the constitution of just wars,
Men, in their eloquent fashion, understood.

Relieved of soul, the dropping-back of dust,
Their usage, pride, admitted within doors;
At home, under caved chantries, set in trust,
With well-dressed alabaster and proved spurs
They lie; they lie; secure in the decay
Of blood, blood-marks, crowns hacked and coveted,
Before the scouring fires of trial-day
Alight on men; before sleeked groin, gored head,
Budge through the clay and gravel, and the sea
Across daubed rock evacuates its dead.

Two Formal Elegies

For the Jews in Europe

I

Knowing the dead, and how some are disposed:
Subdued under rubble, water, in sand graves,
In clenched cinders not yielding their abused
Bodies and bonds to those whom war's chance saves
Without the law: we grasp, roughly, the song.
Arrogant acceptance from which song derives
Is bedded with their blood, makes flourish young
Roots in ashes. The wilderness revives,

Deceives with sweetness harshness. Still beneath
Live skin stone breathes, about which fires but play,
Fierce heart that is the iced brain's to command
To judgment — studied reflex, contained breath —
Their best of worlds since, on the ordained day,
This world went spinning from Jehovah's hand.

2

For all that must be gone through, their long death
Documented and safe, we have enough
Witnesses (our world being witness-proof).
The sea flickers, roars, in its wide hearth.
Here, yearly, the pushing midlanders stand
To warm themselves; men brawny with life,
Women who expect life. They relieve
Their thickening bodies, settle on scraped sand.

Is it good to remind them, on a brief screen,
Of what they have witnessed and not seen?
(Deaths of the city that persistently dies. . . ?)
To put up stones ensures some sacrifice.
Sufficient men confer, carry their weight.
(At whose door does the sacrifice stand or start?)

Metamorphoses

I THE FEAR

No manner of address will do;
Eloquence is not in that look,
But fear of a furred kind. You
Display the stiff face of shock.

Hate is not in it, nor that
Which has presence, a character
In civil intercourse — deceit
Of a tough weathering-nature.

This fear strikes hard and is gone
And is recognized when found
Not only between dark and dawn,
The summit and the ground.

2

Through scant pride to be so put out!
But feed, feed, unlyrical scapegoat;
Plague shrines where each fissure blows
Odour of laurel clouding yours.

Exercise, loftily, your visions
Where the mountainous distance
Echoes its unfaltering speech
To mere outcry and harrowing search.

Possessed of agility and passion,
Energy (out–of–town–fashion)
Attack every obstacle
And height; make the sun your pedestal.

Settle all that bad blood;
Be visited, touched, understood;
Be graced, groomed, returned to favour
With admirable restraint and fervour.

3 THE RE-BIRTH OF VENUS

And now the sea-scoured temptress, having failed
To scoop out of horizons what birds herald:
Tufts of fresh soil: shakes off an entire sea,
Though not as the dove, harried. Rather, she,

A shark hurricaned to estuary-water,
(The lesser hunter almost by a greater
Devoured) but unflurried, lies, approaches all
Stayers, and searchers of the fanged pool.

Those varied dead. The undiscerning sea
Shelves and dissolves their flesh as it burns spray

Who do not shriek like gulls nor dolphins ride
Crouched under spume to England's erect side

Though there a soaked sleeve lolls or shoe patrols
Tide-padded thick shallows, squats in choked pools

Neither our designed wreaths nor used words
Sink to their melted ears and melted hearts.

5

Doubtless he saw some path clear, having found
His love now fenced him off from the one ground
Where, as he owned, no temperate squalls could move
Either from the profession of their love.

Storm-bound, now she'd outweather him, though he,
Between sun-clouded marshworld and strewn sea
Pitched to extremities, in the rock's vein
Gripped for the winds to roughen and tide stain.

But when he tore his flesh-root and was gone,
Leaving no track, no blood gritting the stone,
Drawn freely to the darkness he had fought
Driven by sulphurous blood and a clenched heart,

Grant the detached, pierced spirit could plunge, soar,
Seeking that love flesh dared not answer for,
Nor suffers now, hammocked in salt tagged cloth
That to be bleached or burned the sea casts out.

Picture of a Nativity

Sea-preserved, heaped with sea-spoils,
Ribs, keels, coral sores,
Detached faces, ephemeral oils,
Discharged on the world's outer shores,

A dumb child-king
Arrives at his right place; rests,
Undisturbed, among slack serpents; beasts
With claws flesh-buttered. In the gathering

Of bestial and common hardship
Artistic men appear to worship
And fall down; to recognize
Familiar tokens; believe their own eyes.

Above the marvel, each rigid head,
Angels, their unnatural wings displayed,
Freeze into an attitude
Recalling the dead.

Canticle for Good Friday

The cross staggered him. At the cliff-top
Thomas, beneath its burden, stood
While the dulled wood
Spat on the stones each drop
Of deliberate blood.

A clamping, cold-figured day
Thomas (not transfigured) stamped, crouched,
Watched
Smelt vinegar and blood. He,
As yet unsearched, unscratched,

And suffered to remain
At such near distance
(A slight miracle might cleanse
His brain
Of all attachments, claw-roots of sense)

In unaccountable darkness moved away,
The strange flesh untouched, carrion-sustenance
Of staunchest love, choicest defiance,
Creation's issue congealing (and one woman's).

The Guardians

The young, having risen early, had gone,
Some with excursions beyond the bay-mouth,
Some toward lakes, a fragile reflected sun.
Thunder-heads drift, awkwardly, from the south;

The old watch them. They have watched the safe
Packed harbours topple under sudden gales,
Great tides irrupt, yachts burn at the wharf
That on clean seas pitched their effective sails.

There are silences. These, too, they endure:
Soft comings-on; soft after-shocks of calm.
Quietly they wade the disturbed shore;
Gather the dead as the first dead scrape home.

The White Ship

Where the living with effort go,
Or with expense, the drowned wander
Easily: seaman
And king's son also

Who, by gross error lost,
Drift, now, in salt crushed
Polyp- and mackerel-fleshed
Tides between coast and coast,

Submerge or half-appear.
This does not much matter.
They are put down as dead. Water
Silences all who would interfere;

Retains, still, what it might give
As casually as it took away:
Creatures passed through the wet sieve
Without enrichment or decay.

Wreaths

1

Each day the tide withdraws; chills us; pastes
The sand with dead gulls, oranges, dead men.
Uttering love, that outlasts or outwastes
Time's attrition, exiles appear again,
But faintly altered in eyes and skin.

2

Into what understanding all have grown!
(Setting aside a few things, the still faces,
Climbing the phosphorus tide, that none will own)
What paradises and watering-places,
What hurts appeased by the sea's handsomeness!

Elegiac Stanzas
On a Visit to Dove Cottage

To J. P. Mann

Mountains, monuments, all forms
Inured to processes and storms
(And they are many); the fashions
Of intercourse between nations:

Customs through which many come
To sink their eyes into a room
Filled with the unused and unworn;
To bite nothings to the bone:

And the daylight between facts;
And the daylight between acts;
Groping of custom towards love;
Past loving, the custom to approve:

A use of words; a rhetoric
As plain as spitting on a stick;
Speech from the ice, the clear-obscure;
The tongue broody in the jaw:

Greatly-aloof, alert, rare
Spirit, conditioned to appear
At the authentic stone or seat:
O near-human spouse and poet,

Mountains, rivers, and grand storms,
Continuous profit, grand customs
(And many of them): O Lakes, Lakes!
O Sentiment upon the rocks!

After Cumae

The sun again unearthed, colours come up fresh,
The perennials; and the laurels'
Washable leaves, that seem never to perish,
Obscure the mouthy cave, the dumb grottoes.

From the beginning, in the known world, slide
Drawn echoing hulls, axes grate, and waves
Deposit in their shallow margins varied
Fragments of marine decay and waftage;

And the sometimes-abandoned gods confuse
With immortal essences men's brief lives,
Frequenting the exposed and pious: those
Who stray, as designed, under applied perils,

Whose doom is easy, venturing so far
Without need, other than to freeze or burn,
Their wake, on spread-out oceans, a healed scar
Fingered, themselves the curios of voyage.

Little Apocalypse
Hölderlin: 1770–1843

Abrupt tempter; close enough to survive
The sun's primitive renewing fury;
Scorched vistas where crawl the injured and brave:
This man stands sealed against their injury:

Hermetic radiance of great suns kept in:
Man's common nature suddenly too rare:
See, for the brilliant coldness of his skin,
The god cast, perfected, among fire.

The Bibliographers

Lucifer blazing in superb effigies
Among the world's ambitious tragedies,
Heaven-sent gift to the dark ages,

Now, in the finest-possible light,
We approach you; can estimate
Your not unnatural height.

Though the discrete progeny,
Out of their swim, go deflated and dry,
We know the feel of you, archaic beauty,

Between the tombs, where the tombs still extrude,
Overshadowing the sun-struck world:
(The shadow-god envisaged in no cloud).

Of Commerce and Society
Variations on a Theme

Then hang this picture for a calendar,
As sheep for goat, and pray most fixedly
For the cold martial progress of your star,
With thoughts of commerce and society,
Well-milked Chinese, Negroes who cannot sing,
The Huns gelded and feeding in a ring.

ALLEN TATE: More Sonnets at Christmas, 1942

I   THE APOSTLES: VERSAILLES, 1919

They sat. They stood about.
They were estranged. The air,
As water curdles from clear,
Fleshed the silence. They sat.

They were appalled. The bells
In hollowed Europe spilt
To the gods of coin and salt.
The sea creaked with worked vessels.

Europe, the much-scarred, much-scoured terrain,
Its attested liberties, home-produce,
Labelled and looking up, invites use,
Stuffed with artistry and substantial gain:

Shrunken, magnified (nest, holocaust)
Not half innocent and not half undone;
Profiting from custom: its replete strewn
Cities such ample monuments to lost

Nations and generations: its cultural
Or trade skeletons such hand-picked bone:
Flaws in the best, revised science marks down:
Witness many devices; the few natural

Corruptions, graftings; witness classic falls
(The dead subtracted; the greatest resigned);
Witness earth fertilized, decently drained,
The sea decent again behind walls.

3 THE DEATH OF SHELLEY

i

Slime; the residues of refined tears;
And, salt-bristled, blown on a drying sea,
The sunned and risen faces.

                    There's Andromeda
Depicted in relief, after the fashion.

'His guarded eyes under his shielded brow'
Through poisonous baked sea-things Perseus
Goes — clogged sword, clear, aimless mirror —
With nothing to strike at or blind
                      in the frothed shallows.

ii

Rivers bring down. The sea
Brings away;
Voids, sucks back, its pearls and auguries.
Eagles or vultures churn the fresh-made skies.

Over the statues, unchanging features
Of commerce and quaint love, soot lies.
Earth steams. The bull and the great mute swan
Strain into life with their notorious cries.

4

Statesmen have known visions. And, not alone,
Artistic men prod dead men from their stone:
Some of us have heard the dead speak:
The dead are my obsession this week

But may be lifted away. In summer
Thunder may strike, or, as a tremor
Of remote adjustment, pass on the far side
From us: however deified and defied

By those it does strike. Many have died. Auschwitz,
Its furnace chambers and lime pits
Half-erased, is half-dead; a fable
Unbelievable in fatted marble.

There is, at times, some need to demonstrate
Jehovah's touchy methods that create
The connoisseur of blood, the smitten man.
At times it seems not common to explain.

5 ODE ON THE LOSS OF THE 'TITANIC'

Thriving against façades the ignorant sea
Souses our public baths, statues, waste ground:
Archaic earth-shaker, fresh enemy
('The tables of exchange being overturned');

Drowns Babel in upheaval and display;
Unswerving, as were the admired multitudes
Silenced from time to time under its sway.
By all means let us appease the terse gods.

Homage to Henry James
'But then face to face'

Naked, as if for swimming, the martyr
Catches his death in a little flutter
Of plain arrows. A grotesque situation,
But priceless, and harmless to the nation.

Consider such pains 'crystalline': then fine art
Persists where most crystals accumulate.
History can be scraped clean of its old price.
Engrossed in the cold blood of sacrifice

The provident and self-healing gods
Destroy only to save. Well-stocked with foods,
Enlarged and deep-oiled, America
Detects music, apprehends the day-star

Where, sensitive and half-under a cloud,
Europe muddles her dreaming, is loud
And critical beneath the varied domes
Resonant with tribute and with commerce.

Doctor Faustus

For it must needs be that offences come; but woe to
that man by whom the offence cometh.

I   THE EMPEROR'S CLOTHES

A way of many ways: a god
Spirals in the pure steam of blood.
And gods — as men — rise from shut tombs
To a disturbance of small drums;

Immaculate plumage of the swan
The common wear. There is no-one
Afraid or overheard, no loud
Voice (though innocently loud).

2   THE HARPIES

Having stood hungrily apart
From the gods' politic banquet,
Of all possible false gods
I fall to these gristled shades

That show everything, without lust;
And stumble upon their dead feast
By the torn *Warning To Bathers*
By the torn waters.

The Innocents have not flown;
Too legendary, they laugh;
The lewd uproarious wolf
Brings their house down.

A beast is slain, a beast thrives.
Fat blood squeaks on the sand.
A blinded god believes
That he is not blind.

A Pastoral

Mobile, immaculate and austere,
The Pities, their fingers in every wound,
Assess the injured on the obscured frontier;
Cleanse with a kind of artistry the ground
Shared by War. Consultants in new tongues
Prove synonymous our separated wrongs.

We celebrate, fluently and at ease.
Traditional Furies, having thrust, hovered,
Now decently enough sustain Peace.
The unedifying nude dead are soon covered.
Survivors, still given to wandering, find
Their old loves, painted and re-aligned —

Queer, familiar, fostered by superb graft
On treasured foundations, these ideal features.
Men can move with purpose again, or drift,
According to direction. Here are statues
Darkened by laurel; and evergreen names;
Evidently-veiled griefs; impervious tombs.

Orpheus and Eurydice

Though there are wild dogs
    Infesting the roads
We have recitals, catalogues
    Of protected birds;

And the rare pale sun
    To water our days.
Men turn to savagery now or turn
    To the laws'

Immutable black and red.
    To be judged for his song,
Traversing the still-moist dead,
    The newly-stung,

Love goes, carrying compassion
    To the rawly-difficult;
His countenance, his hands' motion,
    Serene even to a fault.

In Piam Memoriam

Created purely from glass the saint stands,
Exposing his gifted quite empty hands
Like a conjurer about to begin,
A righteous man begging of righteous men.

2

In the sun lily-and-gold-coloured,
Filtering the cruder light, he has endured,
A feature for our regard; and will keep;
Of worldly purity the stained archetype.

3

The scummed pond twitches. The great holly-tree,
Emptied and shut, blows clear of wasting snow,
The common, puddled substance: beneath,
Like a revealed mineral, a new earth.

To the (Supposed) Patron

Prodigal of loves and barbecues,
Expert in the strangest faunas, at home
He considers the lilies, the rewards.
There is no substitute for a rich man.
At his first entering a new province
With new coin, music, the barest glancing
Of steel or gold suffices. There are many
Tremulous dreams secured under that head.
For his delight and his capacity
To absorb, freshly, the inside–succulence
Of untoughened sacrifice, his bronze agents
Speculate among convertible stones
And drink desert sand. That no mirage
Irritate his mild gaze, the lewd noonday
Is housed in cool places, and fountains
Salt the sparse haze. His flesh is made clean.
For the unfallen — the firstborn, or wise
Councillor — prepared vistas extend
As far as harvest; and idyllic death
Where fish at dawn ignite the powdery lake.

KING LOG

Ovid in the Third Reich

non peccat, quaecumque potest peccasse negare,
solaque famosam culpa professa facit.

Amores, III, xiv

I love my work and my children. God
Is distant, difficult. Things happen.
Too near the ancient troughs of blood
Innocence is no earthly weapon.

I have learned one thing: not to look down
So much upon the damned. They, in their sphere,
Harmonize strangely with the divine
Love. I, in mine, celebrate the love-choir.

Annunciations

The Word has been abroad, is back, with a tanned look
From its subsistence in the stiffening-mire.
Cleansing has become killing, the reward
Touchable, overt, clean to the touch.
Now at a distance from the steam of beasts,
The loathly neckings and fat shook spawn
(Each specimen-jar fed with delicate spawn)
The searchers with the curers sit at meat
And are satisfied. Such precious things put down
And the flesh eased through turbulence the soul
Purples itself; each eye squats full and mild
While all who attend to fiddle or to harp
For betterment, flavour their decent mouths
With gobbets of the sweetest sacrifice.

2

O Love, subject of the mere diurnal grind,
Forever being pledged to be redeemed,
Expose yourself for charity; be assured
The body is but husk and excrement.
Enter these deaths according to the law,
O visited women, possessed sons. Foreign lusts
Infringe our restraints; the changeable
Soldiery have their goings-out and comings-in
Dying in abundance. Choicest beasts
Suffuse the gutters with their colourful blood.
Our God scatters corruption. Priests, martyrs,
Parade to this imperious theme: 'O Love,
You know what pains succeed; be vigilant; strive
To recognize the damned among your friends.'

Locust Songs

To Allan Seager

THE EMBLEM

So with sweet oaths converting the salt earth
To yield, our fathers verged on Paradise:
Each to his own portion of Paradise,
Stung by the innocent venoms of the earth.

GOOD HUSBANDRY

Out of the foliage of sensual pride
Those teeming apples. Summer burned well
The dramatic flesh; made work for pride
Forking into the tender mouths of Hell

Heaped windfalls, pulp for the Gadarene
Squealers. This must be our reward:
To smell God writhing over the rich scene.
Gluttons for wrath, we stomach our reward.

SHILOH CHURCH, 1862:
TWENTY-THREE THOUSAND

O stamping-ground of the shod Word! So hard
On the heels of the damned red-man we came,
Geneva's tribe, outlandish and abhorred —
Bland vistas milky with Jehovah's calm —

Who fell to feasting Nature, the glare
Of buzzards circling; cried to the grim sun
'Jehovah punish us!'; who went too far;
In deserts dropped the odd white turds of bone;

Whose passion was to find out God in this
His natural filth, voyeur of sacrifice, a slow
Bloody unearthing of the God-in-us.
But with what blood, and to what end, Shiloh?

I Had Hope When
Violence Was Ceas't

Dawnlight freezes against the east-wire.
The guards cough 'raus! 'raus! We flinch and grin,
Our flesh oozing towards its last outrage.
That which is taken from me is not mine.

September Song

born 19.6.32 — deported 24.9.42

Undesirable you may have been, untouchable
you were not. Not forgotten
or passed over at the proper time.

As estimated, you died. Things marched,
sufficient, to that end.
Just so much Zyklon and leather, patented
terror, so many routine cries.

(I have made
an elegy for myself it
is true)

September fattens on vines. Roses
flake from the wall. The smoke
of harmless fires drifts to my eyes.

This is plenty. This is more than enough.

An Order of Service

He was the surveyor of his own ice-world,
Meticulous at the chosen extreme,
Though what he surveyed may have been nothing.

Let a man sacrifice himself, concede
His mortality and have done with it;
There is no end to that sublime appeal.

In such a light dismiss the unappealing
Blank of his gaze, hopelessly vigilant,
Dazzled by renunciation's glare.

The Humanist

The *Venice* portrait: he
Broods, the achieved guest
Tired and word-perfect
At the Muses' table.

Virtue is virtù. These
Lips debate and praise
Some rich aphorism,
A delicate white meat.

The commonplace hands once
Thick with Plato's blood
(Tasteless! tasteless!) are laid
Dryly against the robes.

Funeral Music

William de la Pole, Duke of Suffolk: beheaded 1450
John Tiptoft, Earl of Worcester: beheaded 1470
Anthony Woodville, Earl Rivers: beheaded 1483

I

Processionals in the exemplary cave,
Benediction of shadows. Pomfret. London.
The voice fragrant with mannered humility,
With an equable contempt for this world,
'In honorem Trinitatis'. Crash. The head
Struck down into a meaty conduit of blood.
So these dispose themselves to receive each
Pentecostal blow from axe or seraph,
Spattering block-straw with mortal residue.
Psalteries whine through the empyrean. Fire
Flares in the pit, ghosting upon stone
Creatures of such rampant state, vacuous
Ceremony of possession, restless
Habitation, no man's dwelling-place.

2

For whom do we scrape our tribute of pain —
For none but the ritual king? We meditate
A rueful mystery; we are dying
To satisfy fat Caritas, those
Wiped jaws of stone. (Suppose all reconciled
By silent music; imagine the future
Flashed back at us, like steel against sun,
Ultimate recompense.) Recall the cold
Of Towton on Palm Sunday before dawn,
Wakefield, Tewkesbury: fastidious trumpets
Shrilling into the ruck; some trampled
Acres, parched, sodden or blanched by sleet,
Stuck with strange-postured dead. Recall the wind's
Flurrying, darkness over the human mire.

3

They bespoke doomsday and they meant it by
God, their curved metal rimming the low ridge.
But few appearances are like this. Once
Every five hundred years a comet's
Over-riding stillness might reveal men
In such array, livid and featureless,
With England crouched beastwise beneath it all.
'Oh, that old northern business . . .' A field
After battle utters its own sound
Which is like nothing on earth, but is earth.
Blindly the questing snail, vulnerable
Mole emerge, blindly we lie down, blindly
Among carnage the most delicate souls
Tup in their marriage-blood, gasping 'Jesus'.

4

Let mind be more precious than soul; it will not
Endure. Soul grasps its price, begs its own peace,
Settles with tears and sweat, is possibly
Indestructible. That I can believe.
Though I would scorn the mere instinct of faith,
Expediency of assent, if I dared,
What I dare not is a waste history
Or void rule. Averroes, old heathen,
If only you had been right, if Intellect
Itself were absolute law, sufficient grace,
Our lives could be a myth of captivity
Which we might enter: an unpeopled region
Of ever new-fallen snow, a palace blazing
With perpetual silence as with torches.

5

As with torches we go, at wild Christmas,
When we revel in our atonement
Through thirty feasts of unction and slaughter,
What is that but the soul's winter sleep?
So many things rest under consummate
Justice as though trumpets purified law,
Spikenard were the real essence of remorse.
The sky gathers up darkness. When we chant
'Ora, ora pro nobis' it is not
Seraphs who descend to pity but ourselves.
Those righteously-accused those vengeful
Racked on articulate looms indulge us
With lingering shows of pain, a flagrant
Tenderness of the damned for their own flesh:

6

My little son, when you could command marvels
Without mercy, outstare the wearisome
Dragon of sleep, I rejoiced above all —
A stranger well-received in your kingdom.
On those pristine fields I saw humankind
As it was named by the Father; fabulous
Beasts rearing in stillness to be blessed.
The world's real cries reached there, turbulence
From remote storms, rumour of solitudes,
A composed mystery. And so it ends.
Some parch for what they were; others are made
Blind to all but one vision, their necessity
To be reconciled. I believe in my
Abandonment, since it is what I have.

7

'Prowess, vanity, mutual regard,
It seemed I stared at them, they at me.
That was the gorgon's true and mortal gaze:
Averted conscience turned against itself.'
A hawk and a hawk-shadow. 'At noon,
As the armies met, each mirrored the other;
Neither was outshone. So they flashed and vanished
And all that survived them was the stark ground
Of this pain. I made no sound, but once
I stiffened as though a remote cry
Had heralded my name. It was nothing . . .'
Reddish ice tinged the reeds; dislodged, a few
Feathers drifted across; carrion birds
Strutted upon the armour of the dead.

8

Not as we are but as we must appear,
Contractual ghosts of pity; not as we
Desire life but as they would have us live,
Set apart in timeless colloquy.
So it is required; so we bear witness,
Despite ourselves, to what is beyond us,
Each distant sphere of harmony forever
Poised, unanswerable. If it is without
Consequence when we vaunt and suffer, or
If it is not, all echoes are the same
In such eternity. Then tell me, love,
How that should comfort us — or anyone
Dragged half-unnerved out of this worldly place,
Crying to the end 'I have not finished'.

Four Poems Regarding the Endurance of Poets

MEN ARE A MOCKERY OF ANGELS

i.m. Tommaso Campanella, priest and poet

Some days a shadow through
The high window shares my
Prison. I watch a slug
Scale the glinting pit-side
Of its own slime. The cries
As they come are mine; then
God's: my justice, wounds, love,
Derisive light, bread, filth.

To lie here in my strange
Flesh while glutted Torment
Sleeps, stained with its prompt food,
Is a joy past all care
Of the world, for a time.
But we are commanded
To rise, when, in silence,
I would compose my voice.

A PRAYER TO THE SUN

i.m. Miguel Hernandez

i
Darkness
above all things
the Sun
makes
rise

ii
Vultures
salute their meat
at noon
(Hell is
silent)

iii
Blind Sun
our ravager
bless us
so that
we sleep.

'DOMAINE PUBLIC'

i.m. Robert Desnos, died Terezin Camp, 1945

For reading I can recommend
   the Fathers. How they
cultivate the corrupting flesh:

toothsome contemplation: cleanly
   maggots churning spleen
to milk. For exercise, prolonged

suppression of much improper
   speech from proper tombs.
If the ground opens, should men's mouths

open also? 'I am nothing
   if not saved now!' or
'Christ, what a pantomime!' The days

of the week are seven pits. Look,
   Seigneur, again we
resurrect and the judges come.

A Valediction to Osip Mandelstam

Difficult friend, I would have preferred
You to them. The dead keep their sealed lives
And again I am too late. Too late
The salutes, dust-clouds and brazen cries.

Images rear from desolation
Look . . . ruins upon a plain . . .
A few men glare at their hands; others
Grovel for food in the roadside field.

Tragedy has all under regard.
It will not touch us but it is there —
Flawless, insatiate — hard summer sky
Feasting on this, reaching its own end.

The Imaginative Life

Evasive souls, of whom the wise lose track,
Die in each night, who, with their day-tongues, sift
The waking-taste of manna or of blood:

The raw magi, part-barbarians,
Entranced by demons and desert frost,
By the irregular visions of a god,

Suffragans of the true seraphs. Lust
Writhes, is dumb savage and in their way
As a virulence natural to the earth.

Renewed glories batten on the poor bones;
Gargantuan mercies whetted by a scent
Of mortal sweat: as though the sleeping flesh

Adored by Furies, stirred, yawned, were driven
In mid-terror to purging and delight.
As though the dead had *Finis* on their brows.

The Assisi Fragments

To G. Wilson Knight

1

Lion and lioness, the mild
Inflammable beasts,
At their precise peril kept
Distance and repose —
And there the serpent
Innocently shone its head.

2

So the hawk had its pursuit. So Death
Opened its childish eyes. So the angels
Overcame Adam: he was defiled
By balm. Creator, and creature made
Of unnatural earth, he howled
To the raven *find me;* to the wolf
Eat, my brother; and to the fire *I am clean.*

History as Poetry

Poetry as salutation; taste
Of Pentecost's ashen feast. Blue wounds.
The tongue's atrocities. Poetry
Unearths from among the speechless dead

Lazarus mystified, common man
Of death. The lily rears its gouged face
From the provided loam. Fortunate
Auguries; whirrings; tarred golden dung:

'A resurgence' as they say. The old
Laurels wagging with the new: Selah!
Thus laudable the trodden bone thus
Unanswerable the knack of tongues.

Soliloquies

THE STONE MAN

To Charles Causley

Recall, now, the omens of childhood:
The nettle–clump and rank elder–tree;
The stones waiting in the mason's yard:

Half-recognized kingdom of the dead:
A deeper landscape lit by distant
Flashings from their journey. At nightfall

My father scuffed clay into the house.
He set his boots on the bleak iron
Of the hearth; ate, drank, unbuckled, slept.

I leaned to the lamp; the pallid moths
Clipped its glass, made an autumnal sound.
Words clawed my mind as though they had smelt

Revelation's flesh . . . So, with an ease
That is dreadful, I summon all back.
The sun bellows over its parched swarms.

What I lost was not a part of this.
The dark-blistered foxgloves, wet berries
Glinting from shadow, small ferns and stones,

Seem fragments, in the observing mind,
Of its ritual power. Old age
Singles them out as though by first-light,

As though a still-life, preserving some
Portion of the soul's feast, went with me
Everywhere, to be hung in strange rooms,

Loneliness being what it is. If
I knew the exact coin for tribute,
Defeat might be bought, processional

Silence gesture its tokens of earth
At my mouth: as in the great death-songs
Of Propertius (although he died young).

Cowan Bridge

At the site of 'Lowood School'

A lost storm in this temperate place;
The silent direction;
Some ash-trees and foam-patched
Alders at the beck.

All the seasons absorbed
As by a child, safe from rain,
Crouched in the dank
Stench of an elder-bush.

So much that was not justice,
So much that is;
The vulnerable pieties
Not willingly let die;
By chance unmolested
The modesty of her rage.

Fantasia on 'Horbury'

John Bacchus Dykes, 1859

Dry walls, and nettles battered by the dust,
Odours from gathered water, muddled storm-clouds
Disastrous over the manufactured West Riding.

Mind — a fritter of excrement; step
Aside, step aside, sir! Ah, but a priest
In his prime watches where he goes. He goes

To tender his confession. Forgiveness
Journeys towards him like a brisk traveller
On the same road. Is this Horbury?

Yes: and he will perpetuate this refuge.
Yes: and he will weaken, scribbling, at the end,
Of unspeakable desolation. Really? Good Lord!

Consider him thus animated,
That outworn piety and those plush tunes
Restored for the sake of a paradox

And the too-fashionable North. Or, again,
Consider him catspawed by an indolent poem,
This place not of his choosing, this menace

From concave stormlight a freak suggestion . . .
These heads of nettles lopped into the dust . . .

Three Baroque Meditations

I

Do words make up the majesty
Of man, and his justice
Between the stones and the void?

How they watch us, the demons
Plugging their dumb wounds! When
Exorcized they shrivel yet thrive.

An owl plunges to its tryst
With a field-mouse in the sharp night.
My fire squeals and lies still.

Minerva, receive this hard
Praise: I speak well of Death;
I confess to the priest in me;

I am shadowed by the wise bird
Of necessity, the lithe
Paradigm Sleep-and-Kill.

2

Anguish bloated by the replete scream.
Flesh of abnegation: the poem
Moves grudgingly to its extreme form,

Vulnerable, to the lamp's fierce head
Of well-trimmed light. In darkness outside,
Foxes and rain-sleeked stones and the dead —

Aliens of such a theme — endure
Until I could cry 'Death! Death!' as though
To exacerbate that suave power;

But refrain. For I am circumspect,
Lifting the spicy lid of my tact
To sniff at the myrrh. It is perfect

In its impalpable bitterness,
Scent of a further country where worse
Furies promenade and bask their claws.

3   THE DEAD BRIDE

So white I was, he would have me cry
   'Unclean!' murderously
To heal me with far-fetched blood.

I writhed to conceive of him.
I clawed to becalm him.
Some nights, I witnessed his face in sleep

And dreamed of my father's
House. (By day he professed languages —
   Disciplines of languages)

By day I cleansed my thin tongue
From its nightly prowl, its vixen-skill,
   His sacramental mouth

   That justified my flesh
And moved well among women
In nuances and imperatives.

This was the poet of a people's
   Love. I hated him. He weeps,
Solemnizing his loss.

The Songbook of
Sebastian Arrurruz

Sebastian Arrurruz: 1868–1922

I

Ten years without you. For so it happens.
Days make their steady progress, a routine
That is merciful and attracts nobody.

Already, like a disciplined scholar,
I piece fragments together, past conjecture
Establishing true sequences of pain;

For so it is proper to find value
In a bleak skill, as in the thing restored:
The long-lost words of choice and valediction.

COPLAS

'One cannot lose what one has not possessed.'
So much for that abrasive gem.
I can lose what I want. I want you.

ii

Oh my dear one, I shall grieve for you
For the rest of my life with slightly
Varying cadence, oh my dear one.

iii

Half-mocking the half-truth, I note
'The wild brevity of sensual love'.
I am shaken, even by that.

iv

It is to him I write, it is to her
I speak in contained silence. Will they be touched
By the unfamiliar passion between them?

3

What other men do with other women
Is for me neither orgy nor sacrament
Nor a language of foreign candour

But is mere occasion or chance distance
Out of which you might move and speak my name
As I speak yours, bargaining with sleep's

Miscellaneous gods for as much
As I can have: an alien landscape,
The dream where you are always to be found.

4

A workable fancy. Old petulant
Sorrow comes back to us, metamorphosed
And semi-precious. Fortuitous amber.
As though this recompensed our deprivation.
See how each fragment kindles as we turn it,
At the end, into the light of appraisal.

5

Love, oh my love, it will come
Sure enough. A storm
Broods over the dry earth all day.
At night the shutters throb in its downpour.

The metaphor holds; is a snug house.
You are outside, lost somewhere. I find myself
Devouring verses of stranger passion
And exile. The exact words

Are fed into my blank hunger for you.

POSTURES

I imagine, as I imagine us
Each time more stylized more lovingly
Detailed, that I am not myself
But someone I might have been: sexless,
Indulgent about art, relishing
Let us say the well-schooled
Postures of *St Anthony* or *St Jerome,*
Those peaceful hermaphrodite dreams
Through which the excess of memory
Pursues its own abstinence.

FROM THE LATIN

There would have been things to say, quietness
That could feed on our lust, refreshed
Trivia, the occurrences of the day;
And at night my tongue in your furrow.

Without you I am mocked by courtesies
And chat, where satisfied women push
Dutifully toward some unneeded guest
Desirable features of conversation.

A LETTER FROM ARMENIA

So, remotely, in your part of the world:
the ripe glandular blooms, and cypresses
shivering with heat (which we have borne
also, in our proper ways) I turn my mind
towards delicate pillage, the provenance
of shards glazed and unglazed, the three
kinds of surviving grain. I hesitate amid
circumstantial disasters. I gaze at the
authentic dead.

Roughly-silvered leaves that are the snow
On Ararat seen through those leaves.
The sun lays down a foliage of shade.

A drinking-fountain pulses its head
Two or three inches from the troughed stone.
An old woman sucks there, gripping the rim.

Why do I have to relive, even now,
Your mouth, and your hand running over me
Deft as a lizard, like a sinew of water?

TO HIS WIFE

You ventured occasionally —
As though this were another's house —
Not intimate but an acquaintance
Flaunting her modest claim; like one
Idly commiserated by new-mated
Lovers rampant in proper delight
When all their guests have gone.

II

Scarcely speaking: it becomes as a
Coolness between neighbours. Often
There is this orgy of sleep. I wake
To caress propriety with odd words
And enjoy abstinence in a vocation
Of now-almost-meaningless despair.

MERCIAN HYMNS

I

King of the perennial holly-groves, the riven sand-
stone: overlord of the M5: architect of the his-
toric rampart and ditch, the citadel at Tamworth,
the summer hermitage in Holy Cross: guardian of
the Welsh Bridge and the Iron Bridge: contractor
to the desirable new estates: saltmaster: money-
changer: commissioner for oaths: martyrologist:
the friend of Charlemagne.

'I liked that,' said Offa, 'sing it again.'

II

A pet-name, a common name. Best-selling brand, curt
graffito. A laugh; a cough. A syndicate. A specious
gift. Scoffed-at horned phonograph.

The starting-cry of a race. A name to conjure with.

III

On the morning of the crowning we chorused our re-
mission from school. It was like Easter: hankies
and gift-mugs approved by his foreign gaze, the
village-lintels curlered with paper flags.

We gaped at the car-park of 'The Stag's Head' where a
bonfire of beer-crates and holly-boughs whistled
above the tar. And the chef stood there, a king in
his new-risen hat, sealing his ' brisk largesse with
'any mustard?'

IV

I was invested in mother-earth, the crypt of roots
and endings. Child's-play. I abode there, bided my
time: where the mole

shouldered the clogged wheel, his gold solidus; where
dry-dust badgers thronged the Roman flues, the
long-unlooked-for mansions of our tribe.

V

So much for the elves' wergild, the true governance
of England, the gaunt warrior-gospel armoured in
engraved stone. I wormed my way heavenward for
ages amid barbaric ivy, scrollwork of fern.

Exile or pilgrim set me once more upon that ground:
my rich and desolate childhood. Dreamy, smug-faced,
sick on outings — I who was taken to be a king of
some kind, a prodigy, a maimed one.

VI

The princes of Mercia were badger and raven. Thrall
to their freedom, I dug and hoarded. Orchards
fruited above clefts. I drank from honeycombs of
chill sandstone.

'A boy at odds in the house, lonely among brothers.'
But I, who had none, fostered a strangeness; gave
myself to unattainable toys.

Candles of gnarled resin, apple-branches, the tacky
mistletoe. 'Look' they said and again 'look.' But
I ran slowly; the landscape flowed away, back to
its source.

In the schoolyard, in the cloakrooms, the children
boasted their scars of dried snot; wrists and
knees garnished with impetigo.

VII

Gasholders, russet among fields. Milldams, marlpools
that lay unstirring. Eel-swarms. Coagulations of
frogs; once, with branches and half-bricks, he
battered a ditchful; then sidled away from the
stillness and silence.

Ceolred was his friend and remained so, even after
the day of the lost fighter: a biplane, already
obsolete and irreplaceable, two inches of heavy
snub silver. Ceolred let it spin through a hole
in the classroom-floorboards, softly, into the
rat-droppings and coins.

After school he lured Ceolred, who was sniggering
with fright, down to the old quarries, and flayed
him. Then, leaving Ceolred, he journeyed for hours,
calm and alone, in his private derelict sandlorry
named *Albion*.

VIII

The mad are predators. Too often lately they harbour
against us. A novel heresy exculpates all maimed
souls. Abjure it! I am the King of Mercia, and
I know.

Threatened by phone-calls at midnight, venomous let-
ters, forewarned I have thwarted their imminent
devices.

Today I name them; tomorrow I shall express the new
law. I dedicate my awakening to this matter.

IX

The strange church smelled a bit 'high', of censers
and polish. The strange curate was just as ap-
propriate: he took off into the marriage-service.
No-one cared to challenge that gambit.

Then he dismissed you, and the rest of us followed,
sheepish next-of-kin, to the place without the
walls: spoil-heaps of chrysanths dead in their
plastic macs, eldorado of washstand-marble.

Embarrassed, we dismissed ourselves: the three mute
great-aunts borne away down St Chad's Garth in
a stiff-backed Edwardian Rolls.

I unburden the saga of your burial, my dear. You had
lived long enough to see things 'nicely settled'.

X

He adored the desk, its brown-oak inlaid with ebony, assorted prize pens, the seals of gold and base metal into which he had sunk his name.

It was there that he drew upon grievances from the people; attended to signatures and retributions; forgave the death-howls of his rival. And there he exchanged gifts with the Muse of History.

What should a man make of remorse, that it might profit his soul? Tell me. Tell everything to Mother, darling, and God bless.

He swayed in sunlight, in mild dreams. He tested the little pears. He smeared catmint on his palm for his cat Smut to lick. He wept, attempting to master *ancilla* and *servus*.

XI

Coins handsome as Nero's; of good substance and weight. *Offa Rex* resonant in silver, and the names of his moneyers. They struck with accountable tact. They could alter the king's face.

Exactness of design was to deter imitation; mutilation if that failed. Exemplary metal, ripe for commerce. Value from a sparse people, scrapers of salt-pans and byres.

Swathed bodies in the long ditch; one eye upstaring. It is safe to presume, here, the king's anger. He reigned forty years. Seasons touched and retouched the soil.

Heathland, new-made watermeadow. Charlock, marsh-marigold. Crepitant oak forest where the boar furrowed black mould, his snout intimate with worms and leaves.

XII

Their spades grafted through the variably-resistant
soil. They clove to the hoard. They ransacked
epiphanies, vertebrae of the chimera, armour of
wild bees' larvae. They struck the fire-dragon's
faceted skin.

The men were paid to caulk water-pipes. They brewed
and pissed amid splendour; their latrine seethed
its estuary through nettles. They are scattered
to your collations, moldywarp.

It is autumn. Chestnut-boughs clash their inflamed
leaves. The garden festers for attention: telluric
cultures, enriched with shards, corms, nodules, the
sunk solids of gravity. I have raked up a golden
and stinking blaze.

XIII

Trim the lamp; polish the lens; draw, one by one, rare
coins to the light. Ringed by its own lustre, the
masterful head emerges, kempt and jutting, out of
England's well. Far from his underkingdom of crin-
oid and crayfish, the rune-stone's province, *Rex
Totius Anglorum Patriae,* coiffured and ageless,
portrays the self-possession of his possession,
cushioned on a legend.

XIV

Dismissing reports and men, he put pressure on the wax, blistered it to a crest. He threatened malefactors with ash from his noon cigar.

When the sky cleared above Malvern, he lingered in his orchard; by the quiet hammer-pond. Trout-fry simmered there, translucent, as though forming the water's underskin. He had a care for natural minutiae. What his gaze touched was his tenderness. Woodlice sat pellet-like in the cracked bark and a snail sugared its new stone.

At dinner, he relished the mockery of drinking his family's health. He did this whenever it suited him, which was not often.

XV

Tutting, he wrenched at a snarled root of dead crab-
apple. It rose against him. In brief cavort he was
Cernunnos, the branched god, lightly concussed.

He divided his realm. It lay there like a dream. An
ancient land, full of strategy. Ramparts of com-
post pioneered by red-helmeted worms. Hemlock in
ambush, night-soil, tetanus. A wasps' nest en-
sconced in the hedge-bank, a reliquary or wrapped
head, the corpse of Cernunnos pitching dayward
its feral horns.

XVI

Clash of salutation. As keels thrust into shingle.
Ambassadors, pilgrims. What is carried over? The
Frankish gift, two-edged, regaled with slaughter.

The sword is in the king's hands; the crux a crafts-
man's triumph. Metal effusing its own fragrance,
a variety of balm. And other miracles, other
exchanges.

Shafts from the winter sun homing upon earth's rim.
Christ's mass: in the thick of a snowy forest the
flickering evergreen fissured with light.

Attributes assumed, retribution entertained. What is
borne amongst them? Too much or too little. In-
dulgences of bartered acclaim; an expenditure, a
hissing. Wine, urine and ashes.

XVII

He drove at evening through the hushed Vosges. The
car radio, glimmering, received broken utterance
from the horizon of storms . . .

'God's honour — our bikes touched; he skidded and came
off.' 'Liar.' A timid father's protective bellow.
Disfigurement of a village-king. 'Just look at
the bugger . . .'

His maroon GT chanted then overtook. He lavished on
the high valleys its *haleine*.

XVIII

At Pavia, a visitation of some sorrow. Boethius'
dungeon. He shut his eyes, gave rise to a tower
out of the earth. He willed the instruments of
violence to break upon meditation. Iron buckles
gagged; flesh leaked rennet over them; the men
stooped, disentangled the body.

He wiped his lips and hands. He strolled back to the
car, with discreet souvenirs for consolation and
philosophy. He set in motion the furtherance of
his journey. To watch the Tiber foaming out
much blood.

XIX

Behind the thorn-trees thin smoke, scutch-grass or wattle smouldering. At this distance it is hard to tell. Far cries impinge like the faint tinking of iron.

We have a kitchen-garden riddled with toy-shards, with splinters of habitation. The children shriek and scavenge, play havoc. They incinerate boxes, rags and old tyres. They haul a sodden log, hung with soft shields of fungus, and launch it upon the flames.

XX

Primeval heathland spattered with the bones of mice and birds; where adders basked and bees made provision, mantling the inner walls of their burh:

Coiled entrenched England: brickwork and paintwork stalwart above hacked marl. The clashing primary colours — 'Ethandune', 'Catraeth', 'Maldon', 'Pengwern'. Steel against yew and privet. Fresh dynasties of smiths.

XXI

Cohorts of charabancs fanfared Offa's province and
his concern, negotiating the by-ways from Teme
to Trent. Their windshields dripped butterflies.
Stranded on hilltops they signalled with plumes
of steam. Twilight menaced the land. The young
women wept and surrendered.

Still, everyone was cheerful, heedless in such days:
at summer weekends dipping into valleys beyond
Mercia's dyke. Tea was enjoyed, by lakesides where
all might fancy carillons of real Camelot vi-
brating through the silent water.

Gradually, during the years, deciduous velvet peeled
from evergreen albums and during the years more
treasures were mislaid: the harp-shaped brooches,
the nuggets of fool's gold.

XXII

We ran across the meadow scabbed with cow-dung, past
the crab-apple trees and camouflaged nissen hut.
It was curfew-time for our war-band.

At home the curtains were drawn. The wireless boomed
its commands. I loved the battle-anthems and the
gregarious news.

Then, in the earthy shelter, warmed by a blue-glassed
storm-lantern, I huddled with stories of dragon-
tailed airships and warriors who took wing im-
mortal as phantoms.

XXIII

In tapestries, in dreams, they gathered, as it was en-
acted, the return, the re-entry of transcendence
into this sublunary world. *Opus Anglicanum,* their
stringent mystery riddled by needles: the silver
veining, the gold leaf, voluted grape-vine, master-
works of treacherous thread.

They trudged out of the dark, scraping their boots
free from lime-splodges and phlegm. They munched
cold bacon. The lamps grew plump with oily re-
liable light.

XXIV

Itinerant through numerous domains, of his lord's
retinue, to Compostela. Then home for a lifetime
amid West Mercia this master-mason as I envisage
him, intent to pester upon tympanum and chancel-
arch his moody testament, confusing warrior with
lion, dragon-coils, tendrils of the stony vine.

Where best to stand? Easter sunrays catch the ob-
lique face of Adam scrumping through leaves; pale
spree of evangelists and, there, a cross Christ
mumming child Adam out of Hell

('Et exspecto resurrectionem mortuorum' dust in the
eyes, on clawing wings, and lips)

XXV

Brooding on the eightieth letter of *Fors Clavigera,*
I speak this in memory of my grandmother, whose
childhood and prime womanhood were spent in the
nailer's darg.

The nailshop stood back of the cottage, by the fold.
It reeked stale mineral sweat. Sparks had furred
its low roof. In dawn-light the troughed water
floated a damson-bloom of dust —

not to be shaken by posthumous clamour. It is one
thing to celebrate the 'quick forge', another
to cradle a face hare-lipped by the searing wire.

Brooding on the eightieth letter of *Fors Clavigera,*
I speak this in memory of my grandmother, whose
childhood and prime womanhood were spent in the
nailer's darg.

XXVI

Fortified in their front parlours, at Yuletide men
are the more murderous. Drunk, they defy battle-
axes, bellow of whale-bone and dung.

Troll-wives, groaners in sweetness, tooth-bewitchers,
you too must purge for the surfeit of England —
who have scattered peppermint and confetti, your
hundreds-and-thousands.

XXVII

'Now when King Offa was alive and dead', they were all there, the funereal gleemen: papal legate and rural dean; Merovingian car-dealers, Welsh mercenaries; a shuffle of house-carls.

He was defunct. They were perfunctory. The ceremony stood acclaimed. The mob received memorial vouchers and signs.

After that shadowy, thrashing midsummer hail-storm, Earth lay for a while, the ghost-bride of livid Thor, butcher of strawberries, and the shire-tree dripped red in the arena of its uprooting.

XXVIII

Processes of generation; deeds of settlement. The urge to marry well; wit to invest in the properties of healing-springs. Our children and our children's children, o my masters.

Tracks of ancient occupation. Frail ironworks rusting in the thorn-thicket. Hearthstones; charred lullabies. A solitary axe-blow that is the echo of a lost sound.

Tumult recedes as though into the long rain. Groves of legendary holly; silverdark the ridged gleam.

XXIX

'Not strangeness, but strange likeness. Obstinate, outclassed forefathers, I too concede, I am your staggeringly-gifted child.'

So, murmurous, he withdrew from them. Gran lit the gas, his dice whirred in the ludo-cup, he entered into the last dream of Offa the King.

XXX

And it seemed, while we waited, he began to walk to-
    wards us   he vanished

he left behind coins, for his lodging, and traces of
    red mud.

TENEBRAE

The Pentecost Castle

It is terrible to desire and not
possess, and terrible to possess
and not desire.

W. B. YEATS

What we love in other human
beings is the hoped-for satisfaction
of our desire. We do not love their
desire. If what we loved in them
was their desire, then we should
love them as ourself.

SIMONE WEIL

I

They slew by night
upon the road
Medina's pride
Olmedo's flower

Shadows warned him
not to go
not to go
along that road

weep for your lord
Medina's pride
Olmedo's flower
there in the road

2

Down in the orchard
I met my death
under the briar rose
I lie slain

I was going
to gather flowers
my love waited
among the trees

down in the orchard
I met my death
under the briar rose
I lie slain

3

You watchers on the wall
grown old with care
I too looked from the wall
I shall look no more

tell us what you saw
the lord I sought to serve
caught in the thorn grove
his blood on his brow

you keepers of the wall
what friend or enemy
sets free the cry
of the bell

4

At dawn the Mass
burgeons from stone
a Jesse tree
of resurrection

budding with candle
flames the gold
and the white wafers
of the feast

and ghosts for love
void a few tears
of wax upon
forlorn altars

5

Goldfinch and hawk
and the grey aspen tree
I have run to the river
mother call me home

the leaves glint in the wind
turning their quiet song
the wings flash and are still
I sleep in the shade

when I cried out you
made no reply
tonight I shall pass by
without a sound

6

Slowly my heron flies
pierced by the blade
mounting in slow pain
strikes the air with its cries

goes seeking the high rocks
where no man can climb
where the wild balsam stirs
by the little stream

the rocks the high rocks
are brimming with flowers
there love grows and there love
rests and is saved

7

I went out early
to the far field
ermine and lily
and yet a child

Love stood before me
in that place
prayers could not lure me
to Christ's house

Christ the deceiver
took all I had
his darkness ever
my fair reward

8

And you my spent heart's treasure
my yet unspent desire
measurer past all measure
cold paradox of fire

as seeker so forsaken
consentingly denied
your solitude a token
the sentries at your side

fulfilment to my sorrow
indulgence of your prey
the sparrowhawk the sparrow
the nothing that you say

9

This love will see me dead
he has the place in mind
where I am free to die
be true at last true love

my love meet me half-way
I bear no sword of fear
where you dwell I
dwell also says my lord

dealing his five wounds
so cunning and so true
of love to rouse this death
I die to sleep in love

10

St James and St John
bless the road she has gone
St John and St James
a rosary of names

child-beads of fingered bread
never-depleted heart's food
the nominal the real
subsistence past recall

bread we shall never break
love-runes we cannot speak
scrolled effigy of a cry
our passion its display

11

If the night is dark
and the way short
why do you hold back
dearest heart

though I may never
see you again
touch me I will shiver
at the unseen

the night is so dark
the way so short
why do you not break
o my heart

12

Married and not for love
you of all women
you of all women
my soul's darling my love

faithful to my desire
lost in the dream's grasp where
shall I find you everywhere
unmatched in my desire

each of us dispossessed
so richly in my sleep
I rise out of my sleep
crying like one possessed

13

Splendidly-shining darkness
proud citadel of meekness
likening us our unlikeness
majesty of our distress

emptiness ever thronging
untenable belonging
how long until this longing
end in unending song

and soul for soul discover
no strangeness to dissever
and lover keep with lover
a moment and for ever

14

As he is wounded
I am hurt
he bleeds from pride
I from my heart

as he is dying
I shall live
in grief desiring
still to grieve

as he is living
I shall die
sick of forgiving
such honesty

15

I shall go down
to the lovers' well
and wash this wound
that will not heal

beloved soul
what shall you see
nothing at all
yet eye to eye

depths of non-being
perhaps too clear
my desire dying
as I desire

Lachrimae

or

Seven tears figured in seven passionate Pavans

*Passions I allow, and loves I approve, onely
I would wishe that men would alter their
object and better their intent.*
ST ROBERT SOUTHWELL, Marie Magdalens Funeral Teares, 1591

I LACHRIMAE VERAE

Crucified Lord, you swim upon your cross
and never move. Sometimes in dreams of hell
the body moves but moves to no avail
and is at one with that eternal loss.

You are the castaway of drowned remorse,
you are the world's atonement on the hill.
This is your body twisted by our skill
into a patience proper for redress.

I cannot turn aside from what I do;
you cannot turn away from what I am.
You do not dwell in me nor I in you

however much I pander to your name
or answer to your lords of revenue,
surrendering the joys that they condemn.

Splendour of life so splendidly contained,
brilliance made bearable. It is the east
light's embodiment, fit to be caressed,
the god Amor with his eyes of diamond,

celestial worldliness on which has dawned
intelligence of angels, Midas' feast,
the stony hunger of the dispossessed
locked into Eden by their own demand.

Self-love, the slavish master of this trade,
conquistador of fashion and remark,
models new heavens in his masquerade,

its images intense with starry work,
until he tires and all that he has made
vanishes in the chaos of the dark.

3 MARTYRIUM

The Jesus-faced man walking crowned with flies
who swats the roadside grass or glances up
at the streaked gibbet with its birds that swoop,
who scans his breviary while the sweat dries,

fades, now, among the fading tapestries,
brooches of crimson tears where no eyes weep,
a mouth unstitched into a rimless cup,
torn clouds the cauldrons of the martyrs' cries.

Clamorous love, its faint and baffled shout,
its grief that would betray him to our fear,
he suffers for our sake, or does not hear

above the hiss of shadows on the wheat.
Viaticum transfigures earth's desire
in rising vernicles of summer air.

Crucified Lord, however much I burn
to be enamoured of your paradise,
knowing what ceases and what will not cease,
frightened of hell, not knowing where to turn,

I fall between harsh grace and hurtful scorn.
You are the crucified who crucifies,
self-withdrawn even from your own device,
your trim-plugged body, wreath of rakish thorn.

What grips me then, or what does my soul grasp?
If I grasp nothing what is there to break?
You are beyond me, innermost true light,

uttermost exile for no exile's sake,
king of our earth not caring to unclasp
its void embrace, the semblance of your quiet.

5 PAVANA DOLOROSA

Loves I allow and passions I approve:
Ash-Wednesday feasts, ascetic opulence,
the wincing lute, so real in its pretence,
itself a passion amorous of love.

Self-wounding martyrdom, what joys you have,
true-torn among this fictive consonance,
music's creation of the moveless dance,
the decreation to which all must move.

Self-seeking hunter of forms, there is no end
to such pursuits. None can revoke your cry.
Your silence is an ecstasy of sound

and your nocturnals blaze upon the day.
I founder in desire for things unfound.
I stay amid the things that will not stay.

Crucified Lord, so naked to the world,
you live unseen within that nakedness,
consigned by proxy to the judas-kiss
of our devotion, bowed beneath the gold,

with re-enactments, penances foretold:
scentings of love across a wilderness
of retrospection, wild and objectless
longings incarnate in the carnal child.

Beautiful for themselves the icons fade;
the lions and the hermits disappear.
Triumphalism feasts on empty dread,

fulfilling triumphs of the festal year.
We find you wounded by the token spear.
Dominion is swallowed with your blood.

7 LACHRIMAE AMANTIS

What is there in my heart that you should sue
so fiercely for its love? What kind of care
brings you as though a stranger to my door
through the long night and in the icy dew

seeking the heart that will not harbour you,
that keeps itself religiously secure?
At this dark solstice filled with frost and fire
your passion's ancient wounds must bleed anew.

So many nights the angel of my house
has fed such urgent comfort through a dream,
whispered 'your lord is coming, he is close'

that I have drowsed half-faithful for a time
bathed in pure tones of promise and remorse:
'tomorrow I shall wake to welcome him.'

An Apology for the Revival of Christian Architecture in England

the spiritual, Platonic old England . . .
S. T. COLERIDGE, Anima Poetae

'Your situation', said Coningsby, looking up the green
and silent valley, 'is absolutely poetic.'
'I try sometimes to fancy', said Mr Millbank, with a
rather fierce smile, 'that I am in the New World.'
BENJAMIN DISRAELI, Coningsby

I   QUAINT MAZES

And, after all, it is to them we return.
Their triumph is to rise and be our hosts:
lords of unquiet or of quiet sojourn,
those muddy-hued and midge-tormented ghosts.

On blustery lilac-bush and terrace-urn
bedaubed with bloom Linnaean pentecosts
put their pronged light; the chilly fountains burn.
Religion of the heart, with trysts and quests

and pangs of consolation, its hawk's hood
twitched off for sweet carnality, again
rejoices in old hymns of servitude,

haunting the sacred well, the hidden shrine.
It is the ravage of the heron wood;
it is the rood blazing upon the green.

2 DAMON'S LAMENT FOR HIS CLORINDA, YORKSHIRE 1654

November rips gold foil from the oak ridges.
Dour folk huddle in High Hoyland, Penistone.
The tributaries of the Sheaf and Don
bulge their dull spate, cramming the poor bridges.

The North Sea batters our shepherds' cottages
from sixty miles. No sooner has the sun
swung clear above earth's rim than it is gone.
We live like gleaners of its vestiges

knowing we flourish, though each year a child
with the set face of a tomb-weeper is put down
for ever and ever. Why does the air grow cold

in the region of mirrors? And who is this clown
doffing his mask at the masked threshold
to selfless raptures that are all his own?

High voices in domestic chapels; praise;
praise-worthy feuds; new-burgeoned spires that sprung
crisp-leaved as though from dropping-wells. The young
ferns root among our vitrified tears.

What an elopement that was: the hired chaise
tore through the fir-grove, scattered kinsmen flung
buckshot and bridles, and the tocsin swung
from the tarred bellcote dappled with dove-smears.

Wires tarnish in gilt corridors, in each room
stiff with the bric-a-brac of loss and gain.
Love fled, truly outwitted, through a swirl

of long-laid dust. Today you sip and smile
though still not quite yourself. Guarding its pane
the spider looms against another storm.

Make miniatures of the once-monstrous theme:
the red-coat devotees, mêlées of wheels,
Jagannath's lovers. With indifferent aim
unleash the rutting cannon at the walls

of forts and palaces; pollute the wells.
Impound the memoirs for their bankrupt shame,
fantasies of true destiny that kills
'under the sanction of the English name'.

Be moved by faith, obedience without fault,
the flawless hubris of heroic guilt,
the grace of visitation; and be stirred

by all her god-quests, her idolatries,
in conclave of abiding injuries,
sated upon the stillness of the bride.

Suppose they sweltered here three thousand years
patient for our destruction. There is a greeting
beyond the act. Destiny is the great thing,
true lord of annexation and arrears.

Our law-books overrule the emperors.
The mango is the bride-bed of light. Spring
jostles the flame-tree. But new mandates bring
new images of faith, good subahdars!

The flittering candles of the wayside shrines
melt into dawn. The sun surmounts the dust.
Krishna from Radha lovingly untwines.

Lugging the earth, the oxen bow their heads.
The alien conscience of our days is lost
among the ruins and on endless roads.

Malcolm and Frere, Colebrooke and Elphinstone,
the life of empire like the life of the mind
'simple, sensuous, passionate', attuned
to the clear theme of justice and order, gone.

Gone the ascetic pastimes, the Persian
scholarship, the wild boar run to ground,
the watercolours of the sun and wind.
Names rise like outcrops on the rich terrain,

like carapaces of the Mughal tombs
lop-sided in the rice-fields, boarded-up
near railway-crossings and small aerodromes.

'India's a peacock-shrine next to a shop
selling mangola, sitars, lucky charms,
heavenly Buddhas smiling in their sleep.'

Pitched high above the shallows of the sea
lone bells in gritty belfries do not ring
but coil a far and inward echoing
out of the air that thrums. Enduringly,

fuchsia-hedges fend between cliff and sky;
brown stumps of headstones tamp into the ling
the ruined and the ruinously strong.
Platonic England grasps its tenantry

where wild-eyed poppies raddle tawny farms
and wild swans root in lily-clouded lakes.
Vulnerable to each other the twin forms

of sleep and waking touch the man who wakes
to sudden light, who thinks that this becalms
even the phantoms of untold mistakes.

8 VOCATIONS

While friends defected, you stayed and were sure,
fervent in reason, watchful of each name:
a signet-seal's unostentatious gem
gleams against walnut on the escritoire,

focus of reckoning and judicious prayer.
This is the durable covenant, a room
quietly furnished with stuff of martyrdom,
lit by the flowers and moths from your own shire,

by silvery vistas frothed with convolvulus,
radiance of dreams hardly to be denied.
The twittering pipistrelle, so strange and close,

plucks its curt flight through the moist eventide;
the children thread among old avenues
of snowberries, clear-calling as they fade.

Autumn resumes the land, ruffles the woods
with smoky wings, entangles them. Trees shine
out from their leaves, rocks mildew to moss-green;
the avenues are spread with brittle floods.

Platonic England, house of solitudes,
rests in its laurels and its injured stone,
replete with complex fortunes that are gone,
beset by dynasties of moods and clouds.

It stands, as though at ease with its own world,
the mannerly extortions, languid praise,
all that devotion long since bought and sold,

the rooms of cedar and soft-thudding baize,
tremulous boudoirs where the crystals kissed
in cabinets of amethyst and frost.

Remember how, at seven years, the decrees
were brought home: child-soul must register
for Christ's dole, be allotted its first Easter,
blanch-white and empty, chilled by the lilies,

betrothed among the well-wishers and spies.
Reverend Mother, breakfastless, could feast her
constraint on terracotta and alabaster
and brimstone and the sweets of paradise.

Theology makes good bedside reading. Some
who are lost covet scholastic proof,
subsistence of probation, modest balm.

The wooden wings of justice borne aloof,
we close our eyes to Anselm and lie calm.
All night the cisterns whisper in the roof.

The pigeon purrs in the wood; the wood has gone;
dark leaves that flick to silver in the gust,
and the marsh-orchids and the heron's nest,
goldgrimy shafts and pillars of the sun.

Weightless magnificence upholds the past.
Cement recesses smell of fur and bone
and berries wrinkle in the badger-run
and wiry heath-fern scatters its fresh rust.

'O clap your hands' so that the dove takes flight,
bursts through the leaves with an untidy sound,
plunges its wings into the green twilight

above this long-sought and forsaken ground,
the half-built ruins of the new estate,
warheads of mushrooms round the filter-pond.

Stroke the small silk with your whispering hands,
godmother; nod and nod from the half-gloom;
broochlight intermittent between the fronds,
the owl immortal in its crystal dome.

Along the mantelpiece veined lustres trill,
the clock discounts us with a telling chime.
Familiar ministrants, clerks-of-appeal,
burnish upon the threshold of the dream:

churchwardens in wing-collars bearing scrolls
of copyhold well-tinctured and well-tied.
Your photo-albums loved by the boy-king

preserve in sepia waterglass the souls
of distant cousins, virgin till they died,
and the lost delicate suitors who could sing.

So to celebrate that kingdom: it grows
greener in winter, essence of the year;
the apple-branches musty with green fur.
In the viridian darkness of its yews

it is an enclave of perpetual vows
broken in time. Its truth shows disrepair,
disfigured shrines, their stones of gossamer,
Old Moore's astrology, all hallows,

the squire's effigy bewigged with frost,
and hobnails cracking puddles before dawn.
In grange and cottage girls rise from their beds

by candlelight and mend their ruined braids.
Touched by the cry of the iconoclast,
how the rose-window blossoms with the sun!

Two Chorale-Preludes

On melodies by Paul Celan

I AVE REGINA COELORUM

Es ist ein Land Verloren . . .

There is a land called Lost
at peace inside our heads.
The moon, full on the frost,
vivifies these stone heads.

Moods of the verb 'to stare',
split selfhoods, conjugate
ice-facets from the air,
the light glazing the light.

Look at us, Queen of Heaven.
Our solitudes drift by
your solitudes, the seven
dead stars in your sky.

2 TE LUCIS ANTE TERMINUM

Wir gehen dir, Heimat, ins Garn . . .

Centaury with your staunch bloom
you there alder beech you fern,
midsummer closeness my far home,
fresh traces of lost origin.

Silvery the black cherries hang,
the plum-tree oozes through each cleft
and horse-flies siphon the green dung,
glued to the sweetness of their graft:

immortal transience, a 'kind
of otherness', self-understood,
BE FAITHFUL grows upon the mind
as lichen glimmers on the wood.

A Pre-Raphaelite Notebook

Primroses; salutations; the miry skull
of a half-eaten ram; viscous wounds in earth
opening. What seraphs are afoot.

Gold seraph to gold worm in the pierced slime:
greetings. Advent of power-in-grace. The power
of flies distracts the working of our souls.

Earth's abundance. The God-ejected Word
resorts to flesh, procures carrion, satisfies
its white hunger. Salvation's travesty

a deathless metaphor: the stale head
sauced in original blood; the little feast
foaming with cries of rapture and despair.

Terribilis Est Locus Iste

Gauguin and the Pont-Aven School

Briefly they are amazed. The marigold-fields
mell and shudder and the travellers,
in sudden exile burdened with remote
hieratic gestures, journey to no end

beyond the vivid severance of each day,
strangeness at doors, a different solitude
between the mirror and the window, marked
visible absences, colours of the mind,

marginal angels lightning-sketched in red
chalk on the month's accounts or marigolds
in paint runnily embossed, or the renounced
self-portrait with a seraph and a storm.

Veni Coronaberis

A Garland for Helen Waddell

The crocus armies from the dead
rise up; the realm of love renews
the battle it was born to lose,
though for a time the snows have fled

and old stones blossom in the south
with sculpted vine and psaltery
and half-effaced adultery
the bird-dung dribbling from its mouth;

and abstinence crowns all our care
with martyr-laurels for this day.
Towers and steeples rise away
into the towering gulfs of air.

Florentines

Horses, black–lidded mouths peeled back
to white: well–groomed these warriors ride,
their feuds forgotten, remembered, forgotten . . .
a cavalcade passing, night not far–off;
the stricken faces damnable and serene.

'Christmas Trees'

Bonhoeffer in his skylit cell
bleached by the flares' candescent fall,
pacing out his own citadel,

restores the broken themes of praise,
encourages our borrowed days,
by logic of his sacrifice.

Against wild reasons of the state
his words are quiet but not too quiet.
We hear too late or not too late.

Tenebrae

*He was so tired that he was scarcely able to hear a note of
the songs: he felt imprisoned in a cold region where his brain
was numb and his spirit was isolated.*

1

Requite this angel whose
flushed and thirsting face
stoops to the sacrifice
out of which it arose.
This is the lord Eros
of grief who pities
no one; it is
Lazarus with his sores.

2

And you, who with your soft but searching voice
drew me out of the sleep where I was lost,
who held me near your heart that I might rest
confiding in the darkness of your choice:
possessed by you I chose to have no choice,
fulfilled in you I sought no further quest.
You keep me, now, in dread that quenches trust,
in desolation where my sins rejoice.
As I am passionate so you with pain
turn my desire; as you seem passionless
so I recoil from all that I would gain,
wounding myself upon forgetfulness,
false ecstasies, which you in truth sustain
as you sustain each item of your cross.

3

Veni Redemptor, but not in our time.
Christus Resurgens, quite out of this world.
'Ave' we cry; the echoes are returned.
Amor Carnalis is our dwelling-place.

4

O light of light, supreme delight;
grace on our lips to our disgrace.
Time roosts on all such golden wrists;
our leanness is our luxury.
Our love is what we love to have;
our faith is in our festivals.

5

Stupefying images of grief-in-dream,
succubae to my natural grief of heart,
cling to me, then; you who will not desert
your love nor lose him in some blank of time.
You come with all the licence of her name
to tell me you are mine. But you are not
and she is not. Can my own breath be hurt
by breathless shadows groaning in their game?
It can. The best societies of hell
acknowledge this, aroused by what they know:
consummate rage recaptured there in full
as faithfulness demands it, blow for blow,
and rectitude that mimics its own fall
reeling with sensual abstinence and woe.

6

This is the ash–pit of the lily–fire,
this is the questioning at the long tables,
this is true marriage of the self–in–self,
this is a raging solitude of desire,
this is the chorus of obscene consent,
this is a single voice of purest praise.

7

He wounds with ecstasy. All
the wounds are his own.
He wears the martyr's crown.
He is the Lord of Misrule.
He is the Master of the Leaping Figures,
the motley factions.
Revelling in auguries
he is the Weeper of the Valedictions.

8

Music survives, composing her own sphere,
Angel of Tones, Medusa, Queen of the Air,
and when we would accost her with real cries
silver on silver thrills itself to ice.

THE MYSTERY OF
THE CHARITY OF
CHARLES PÉGUY

Crack of a starting-pistol. Jean Jaurès
dies in a wine-puddle. Who or what stares
through the café-window crêped in powder-smoke?
The bill for the new farce reads *Sleepers Awake*.

History commands the stage wielding a toy gun,
rehearsing another scene. It has raged so before,
countless times; and will do, countless times more,
in the guise of supreme clown, dire tragedian.

In Brutus' name martyr and mountebank
ghost Caesar's ghost, his wounds of air and ink
painlessly spouting. Jaurès' blood lies stiff
on menu-card, shirt-front and handkerchief.

Did Péguy kill Jaurès? Did he incite
the assassin? Must men stand by what they write
as by their camp-beds or their weaponry
or shell-shocked comrades while they sag and cry?

Would Péguy answer — stubbornly on guard
among the *Cahiers,* with his army cape
and steely pince-nez and his hermit's beard,
brooding on conscience and embattled hope?

Truth's pedagogue, braving an entrenched class
of fools and scoundrels, children of the world,
his eyes caged and hostile behind glass —
still Péguy said that Hope is a little child.

Violent contrariety of men and days; calm
juddery bombardment of a silent film
showing such things: its canvas slashed with rain
and St Elmo's fire. Victory of the machine!

The brisk celluloid clatters through the gate;
the cortège of the century dances in the street;
and over and over the jolly cartoon
armies of France go reeling towards Verdun.

2

Rage and regret are tireless to explain
stratagems of the out-manoeuvred man,
the charge and counter-charge. You know the drill,
raw veteran, poet with the head of a bull.

Footslogger of genius, skirmisher with grace
and ill-luck, sentinel of the sacrifice,
without vantage of vanity, though mortal-proud,
defend your first position to the last word.

The sun-tanned earth is your centurion;
you are its tribune. On the hard-won
high places the old soldiers of old France
crowd like good children wrapped in obedience

and sleep, and ready to be taken home.
Whatever that vision, it is not a child's;
it is what a child's vision can become.
Memory, Imagination, harvesters of those fields,

our gifts are spoils, our virtues epitaphs,
our substance is the grass upon the graves.
'Du calme, mon vieux, du calme.' How studiously
one cultivates the sugars of decay,

pâtisserie-tinklings of angels ''sieur-'dame',
the smile of the dead novice in its plush frame,
while greed and disaffection are ingrained
like chalk-dust in the ranklings of the mind.

'Rather the Marne than the *Cahiers.*' True enough,
you took yourself off. Dying, your whole life
fell into place. ''Sieurs-'dames, this is the wall
where he leaned and rested, this is the well

from which he drank.' Péguy, you mock us now.
History takes the measure of your brow
in blank-eyed bronze, brave mediocre work
of *Niclausse, sculpteur,* cornered in the park

among the stout dogs and lame patriots
and all those ghosts, far-gazing in mid-stride,
rising from where they fell, still on parade,
covered in glory and the blood of beetroots.

3

Vistas of richness and reward. The cedar
uprears its lawns of black cirrus. You have found
hundred-fold return though in the land
of exile. You are Joseph the Provider;

and in the fable this is your proper home;
three sides of a courtyard where the bees thrum
in the crimped hedges and the pigeons flirt
and paddle, and sunlight pierces the heart-

shaped shutter-patterns in the afternoon,
shadows of fleurs-de-lys on the stone floors.
Here life is labour and pastime and orison
like something from a simple book of hours;

and immortality, your measured task,
inscribes its antique scars on the new desk
among your relics, bits of ivory quartz
and dented snuffbox won at Austerlitz.

The proofs pile up; the dead are made alive
to their posthumous fame. Here is the archive
of your stewardship; here is your true domaine,
its fields of discourse ripening to the Marne.

Château de Trie is yours, Chartres is yours,
and the carved knight of Gisors with the hound;
Colombey-les-deux-Eglises; St Cyr's
cadres and echelons are yours to command.

Yours is their dream of France, militant-pastoral:
musky red gillyvors, the wicker bark
of clematis braided across old brick
and the slow chain that cranks into the well

morning and evening. It is Domrémy
restored; the mystic strategy of Foch
and Bergson with its time-scent, dour panache
deserving of martyrdom. It is an army

of poets, converts, vine-dressers, men skilled
in wood or metal, peasants from the Beauce,
terse teachers of Latin and those unschooled
in all but the hard rudiments of grace.

Such dreams portend, the dreamer prophesies,
is this not true? Truly, if you are wise,
deny such wisdom; bid the grim bonne-femme
defend your door: 'M'sieur is not at home.'

4

This world is different, belongs to them —
the lords of limit and of contumely.
It matters little whether you go tamely
or with rage and defiance to your doom.

This is your enemies' country which they took
in the small hours an age before you woke,
went to the window, saw the mist-hewn
statues of the lean kine emerge at dawn.

Outflanked again, too bad! You still have pride,
haggard obliquities: those that take remorse
and the contempt of others for a muse,
bound to the alexandrine as to the *Code*

Napoléon. Thus the bereaved soul returns
upon itself, grows resolute at chess,
in war-games hurling dice of immense loss
into the breach; thus punitively mourns.

This is no old Beauce manoir that you keep
but the rue de la Sorbonne, the cramped shop,
its unsold *Cahiers* built like barricades,
its fierce disciples, disciplines and feuds,

the camelot-cry of 'sticks!' As Tharaud says,
'all through your life the sound of broken glass.'
So much for Jaurès murdered in cold pique
by some vexed shadow of the belle époque,

some guignol strutting at the window-frame.
But what of you, Péguy, who came to 'exult',
to be called 'wolfish' by your friends? The guilt
belongs to time; and you must leave on time.

Jaurès was killed blindly, yet with reason:
'let us have drums to beat down his great voice.'
So you spoke to the blood. So, you have risen
above all that and fallen flat on your face

among the beetroots, where we are constrained
to leave you sleeping and to step aside
from the fleshed bayonets, the fusillade
of red-rimmed smoke like stubble being burned;

to turn away and contemplate the working
of the radical soul — instinct, intelligence,
memory, call it what you will — waking
into the foreboding of its inheritance,

its landscape and inner domain; images
of earth and grace. Across Artois the rois-mages
march on Bethlehem; sun-showers fall
slantwise over the kalefield, the canal.

Hedgers and ditchers, quarrymen, thick-shod
curés de campagne, each with his load,
shake off those cares and burdens; they become,
in a bleak visionary instant, seraphim

looking towards Chartres, the spired sheaves,
stone-thronged annunciations, winged ogives
uplifted and uplifting from the winter-gleaned
furrows of that criss-cross-trodden ground.

Or say it is Pentecost: the hawthorn-tree,
set with coagulate magnified flowers of may,
blooms in a haze of light; old chalk-pits brim
with seminal verdure from the roots of time.

Landscape is like revelation; it is both
singular crystal and the remotest things.
Cloud-shadows of seasons revisit the earth,
odourless myrrh borne by the wandering kings.

Happy are they who, under the gaze of God,
die for the 'terre charnelle', marry her blood
to theirs, and, in strange Christian hope, go down
into the darkness of resurrection,

into sap, ragwort, melancholy thistle,
almondy meadowsweet, the freshet-brook
rising and running through small wilds of oak,
past the elder-tump that is the child's castle.

Inevitable high summer, richly scarred
with furze and grief; winds drumming the fame
of the tin legions lost in haystack and stream.
Here the lost are blest, the scarred most sacred:

odd village workshops grimed and peppercorned
in a dust of dead spiders, paper-crowned
sunflowers with the bleached heads of rag dolls,
brushes in aspic, clay pots, twisted nails;

the clinking anvil and clear sheepbell-sound,
at noon and evening, of the angelus;
coifed girls like geese, labourers cap in hand,
and walled gardens espaliered with angels;

solitary bookish ecstasies, proud tears,
proud tears, for the forlorn hope, the guerdon
of Sedan, 'oh les braves gens!', English Gordon
stepping down sedately into the spears.

Patience hardens to a pittance, courage
unflinchingly declines into sour rage,
the cobweb-banners, the shrill bugle-bands
and the bronze warriors resting on their wounds.

These fatal decencies, they make us lords
over ourselves: familial debts and dreads,
keepers of old scores, the kindly ones
telling their beady sous, the child-eyed crones

who guard the votive candles and the faint
invalid's night-light of the sacrament,
a host of lilies and the table laid
for early mass from which you stood aside

to find salvation, your novena cleaving
brusquely against the grain of its own myth,
its truth and justice, to a kind of truth,
a justice hard to justify. 'Having

spoken his mind he'd a mind to be silent.'
But who would credit that, that one talent
dug from the claggy Beauce and returned to it
with love, honour, suchlike bitter fruit?

6

To dispense, with justice; or, to dispense
with justice. Thus the catholic god of France,
with honours all even, honours all, even
the damned in the brazen Invalides of Heaven.

Here there should be a section without words
for military band alone: 'Sambre et Meuse',
the 'Sidi Brahim' or 'Le Roi s'Amuse';
white gloves and monocles and polished swords

and Dreyfus with his buttons off, chalk-faced
but standing to attention, the school prig
caught in some act and properly disgraced.
A puffy satrap prances on one leg

to snap the traitor's sword, his ordered rage
bursting with 'cran et gloire' and gouts of rouge.
The chargers click and shiver. There is no stir
in the drawn ranks, among the hosts of the air,

all draped and gathered by the weird storm-light
cheap wood-engravings cast on those who fought
at Mars-la-Tour, Sedan; or on the men
in the world-famous stories of Jules Verne

or nailed at Golgotha. Drumrap and fife
hit the right note: 'A mort le Juif! Le Juif
à la lanterne!' Serenely the mob howls,
its silent mouthings hammered into scrolls

torn from *Apocalypse*. No wonder why
we fall to violence out of apathy,
redeemed by falling and restored to grace
beyond the dreams of mystic avarice.

But who are 'we', since history is law,
clad in our skins of silver, steel and hide,
or in our rags, with rotten teeth askew,
heroes or knaves as Clio shall decide?

'We' are crucified Pilate, Caiaphas
in his thin soutane and Judas with the face
of a man who has drunk wormwood. We come
back empty-handed from Jerusalem

counting our blessings, honestly admire
the wrath of the peacemakers, for example
Christ driving the money-changers from the temple,
applaud the Roman steadiness under fire.

We are the occasional just men who sit
in gaunt self-judgment on their self-defeat,
the élite hermits, secret orators
of an old faith devoted to new wars.

We are 'embusqués', having no wounds to show
save from the thorns, ecstatic at such pain.
Once more the truth advances; and again
the metaphors of blood begin to flow.

7

Salute us all, Christus with your iron
garlands of poppies and ripe carrion.
No, sleep where you stand; let some boy-officer
take up your vigil with your dungfork spear.

What vigil is this, then, among the polled
willows, cart-shafts uptilted against skies,
translucent rain at jutting calvaries;
on paths that are rutted and broken-walled?

What is this relic fumbled with such care
by mittened fingers in dugout or bomb-
tattered, jangling estaminet's upper room?
The incense from a treasured tabatière,

you watchmen at the Passion. Péguy said
'why do I write of war? Simply because
I have not been there. In time I shall cease
to invoke it.' We still dutifully read

'heureux ceux qui sont morts'. Drawn on the past
these presences endure; they have not ceased
to act, suffer, crouching into the hail
like labourers of their own memorial

or those who worship at its marble rote,
their many names one name, the common 'dur'
built into duration, the endurance of war;
blind Vigil herself, helpless and obdurate.

And yet what sights: Saul groping in the dust
for his broken glasses, or the men far-gone
on the road to Emmaus who saw the ghost.
Commit all this to memory. The line

falters, reforms, vanishes into the smoke
of its own unknowing; mother, dad,
gone in that shell-burst, with the other dead,
'pour la patrie', according to the book.

8

Dear lords of life, stump-toothed, with ragged breath,
throng after throng cast out upon the earth,
flesh into dust, who slowly come to use
dreams of oblivion in lieu of paradise,

push on, push on! — through struggle, exhaustion,
indignities of all kinds, the impious Christian
oratory, 'vos morituri', through berserk fear,
laughing, howling, 'servitude et grandeur'

in other words, in nameless gobbets thrown
up by the blast, names issuing from mouths
of the dying, with their dying breaths.
But rest assured, bristly-brave gentlemen

of Normandie and Loire. Death does you proud,
every heroic commonplace, 'Amor',
'Fidelitas', polished like old armour,
stamped forever into the featureless mud.

Poilus and sous-officiers who plod
to your lives' end, name your own recompense,
expecting nothing but the grace of France,
drawn to her arms, her august plenitude.

The blaze of death goes out, the mind leaps
for its salvation, is at once extinct;
its last thoughts tetter the furrows, distinct
in dawn twilight, caught on the barbed loops.

Whatever strikes and maims us it is not
fate, to our knowledge. En avant, Péguy!
The irony of advancement. Say 'we
possess nothing; try to hold on to that.'

9

There is an ancient landscape of green branches —
true tempérament de droite, you have your wish —
crosshatching twigs and light, goldfinches
among the peppery lilac, the small fish

pencilled into the stream. Ah, such a land
the Ile de France once was. Virelai and horn
wind through the meadows, the dawn-masses sound
fresh triumphs for our Saviour crowned with scorn.

Good governors and captains, by your leave,
you also were sore-wounded but those wars
are ended. Iron men who bell the hours,
marshals of porte-cochère and carriage-drive,

this is indeed perfection, this is the heart
of the mystère. Yet one would not suppose
Péguy's 'defeat', 'affliction', your lost cause.
Old Bourbons view-hallooing for regret

among the cobwebs and the ghostly wine,
you dream of warrior-poets and the Meuse
flowing so sweetly; the androgynous Muse
your priest-confessor, sister-châtelaine.

How the mood swells to greet the gathering storm!
The chestnut trees begin to thresh and cast
huge canisters of blossom at each gust.
Coup de tonnerre! Bismarck is in the room!

Bad memories, seigneurs? Such wraiths appear
on summer evenings when the gnat-swarm spins
a dying moment on the tremulous air.
The curtains billow and the rain begins

its night-long vigil. Sombre heartwoods gleam,
the clocks replenish the small hours' advance
and not a soul has faltered from its trance.
'Je est un autre', that fatal telegram,

floats past you in the darkness, unreceived.
Connoisseurs of obligation, history
stands, a blank instant, awaiting your reply:
'If we but move a finger France is saved!'

10

Down in the river-garden a grey-gold
dawnlight begins to silhouette the ash.
A rooster wails remotely over the marsh
like Mr Punch mimicking a lost child.

At Villeroy the copybook lines of men
rise up and are erased. Péguy's cropped skull
dribbles its ichor, its poor thimbleful,
a simple lesion of the complex brain.

Woefully battered but not too bloody,
smeared by fraternal root-crops and at one
with the fritillary and the veined stone,
having composed his great work, his small body,

for the last rites of truth, whatever they are,
or the Last Judgment which is much the same,
or Mercy, even, with her tears and fire,
he commends us to nothing, leaves a name

for the burial-detail to gather up
with rank and number, personal effects,
the next-of-kin and a few other facts;
his arm over his face as though in sleep

or to ward off the sun: the body's prayer,
the tribute of his true passion, for Chartres
steadfastly cleaving to the Beauce, for her,
the Virgin of innumerable charities.

'Encore plus douloureux et doux.' Note how
sweetness devours sorrow, renders it again,
turns to affliction each more carnal pain.
Whatever is fulfilled is now the law

where law is grace, that grace won by inches,
inched years. The men of sorrows do their stint,
whose golgothas are the moon's trenches,
the sun's blear flare over the salient.

J'accuse! j'accuse! — making the silver prance
and curvet, and the dust-motes jig to war
across the shaky vistas of old France,
the gilt-edged maps of Strasbourg and the Saar.

Low tragedy, high farce, fight for command,
march, counter-march, and come to the salute
at every hole-and-corner burial-rite
bellowed with hoarse dignity into the wind.

Take that for your example! But still mourn,
being so moved: éloge and elegy
so moving on the scene as if to cry
'in memory of those things these words were born.'

Hymns to Our Lady of Chartres

I

Eia, with handbells, jews' harps, risible
tuckets of salutation! Otherwise
gnashing and gnawing sound out your praise.
Salve regina! Visible, invisible,

powers, presences, in and beyond the blue
glass, radiantly-occluded Sion, pour
festal light at the feet of the new poor,
scavengers upon grace, and of your true

servant Péguy who cries out from the crowd
where your bienpensants clatter to adore
la Dame du Pilier and her wooden stare.
The priests go nodding by, dainty and shrewd,

and virgins with trim lamps devoutly oiled,
to do the honours of your mysteries.
Through what straits might we come to worship this,
and kneel before you, and be reconciled,

among the flowering lances, the heathen
gold phalanxes of flame; at the high seats
where Mercy is redeemed from its own threats;
with dumb-struck martyrs trumpeted to heaven?

2

Eia ergo. For this is Sion's twin city
or city-in-law. Across France the great west
windows are full of the sun's holocaust,
the dying blazons of eternity

secured in mazy lead and bevelled stone.
Outside the glass, pigeons rancid as gulls
roost in their stucco-dung on the tiered sills.
The candles blur the air before your throne.

Love is at odds. Your beauty has gone out
so many times; too vividly has flared
through the mild dreams of Herod undeterred.
Your eyes are like the eyes of the devout,

O dulcis Virgo. You are the stained world's
ransom, bear its image, live through your
perpetual exile in its courts of prayer.
'This is the carnal rose that re-enfolds

heaven into earth.' They say you are disposed
to acts of grace: tumblers and holy fools.
Child-saints rejoice you, small immaculate souls,
and mundane sorrows mystically espoused.

3

Redemptrice of all vows and fealties, Dame
de Sous-Terre, pray for us, pitched beneath
your mantle, the limestone and sifted earth
of Beauce. Assoil your lordly vassals; some

mettled by virtue, briskly taking Christ,
and some as captives; those to whom the kiss
of peace was torment in the midst of mass,
those who salute you with a raised fist.

Spes nostra, salve! Your strange countenance
is our remaking. Turn, then, its remote
familial smile upon this Christian rote.
Sly innocence of the blood seized in a trance

by violent knowledge — what it is to know
our strength! Pray for those neophytes who found
in you the source of life, their secret wound.
The seraphim with stark pinions aglow

look blankly at us: we who may be spared,
as well as other ecstasies, the hues
of burning and the damned at their old cries,
your varied mercies, variously adored.

NEW POEMS

Sobieski's Shield

1

The blackberry, white
field-rose, all others
of that family:

steadfast is the word

and the star-gazing planet out of which
lamentation is spun.

2

Overnight as the year
            purple garish-brown
aster chrysanthemum
            signally restored
to a subsistence of slant light
as one would venture
                Justice Equity
or Sobieski's Shield even
                        the names
and what they have about them dark to dark.

Of Coming-into-Being
and Passing-Away

To Aileen Ireland

Rosa sericea: its red
spurs
      blooded with amber
each lit and holy grain
the sun
      makes much of
as of all our shadows —

prodigal ever returning
darkness that in such circuits
reflects diuturnity
             to itself
and to our selves
             yields nothing
finally —

      but by occasion
visions of truth or dreams
as they arise —
            to terms of grace
where grace has surprised us —
the unsustaining
            wondrously sustained

Ritornelli

For Hugh Wood on his 6oth birthday

i
Angel of Tones
                    flame of accord
exacting mercies
                      answerable
to rage as solace

I will have you sing

ii
For so the judgment
passes
        it is not
otherwise
             hereafter
you will see them resolved
in tears
        they shall bear
your crowns of redress

iii
Lost to no thought
of triumph he returns
upon himself goes down
among water and ash
and wailing sounds confused
with sounds of joy

Canaan

I

They march at God's
pleasure through Flanders
with machine-pistols,
chorales, cannon

of obese bronze,
with groaning pushcarts,
to topple Baal. At
crossroads they hoist

corpses and soiled
banners of the Lamb.
The sun takes assize.
Aloof the blades

of oblation
rise, fall, as though they
were not obstructed
by blades of bone.

II

Iniquity passes
and rectitude.
They do not spare
the sucking child nor are they
sparing with trumpets.
Now it is
Moloch his ovens
and the dropped babes naked
swung by an arm
or a leg like flails.

Respublica

The strident high
civic trumpeting
of misrule. It is
what we stand for.

Wild insolence,
aggregates without
distinction. Courage
of common men:

spent in the ruck
their remnant witness
after centuries
is granted them

like a pardon.
And other fealties
other fortitudes
broken as named —

Respublica
brokenly recalled,
its archaic laws
and hymnody;

and destroyed hope
that so many times
is brought with triumph
back from the dead.

Song Contest

After Anne Hébert, 'Les Offensés'

By order of hunger the starving stood in line
by dint of wrath the traitors were arraigned
by virtue of conscience the judges came to trial
by scale of offence the injured lay accused
by score of wounds the crucified made their mark
the forlorn hope the final wretchedness
the dumb possessed the barricades en masse
their speechless cry so stridently proclaimed
the Oath took arms against them street on street
its standards were the heavy rods of charge
in lieu of words the one word fire
blazed from its heart

De Jure Belli ac Pacis

i.m. Hans-Bernd von Haeften, 1905–1944

I

The people moves as one spirit unfettered
claim our assessors of stone.
                              When the nations
fall dispossessed such conjurings possess them,
elaborate barren fountains, projected
aqueducts
                where water is no longer found.
Where would one find Grotius for that matter,
the secular justice clamant among psalms,
huge-fisted visionary Comenius . . . ?
Could none predict these haughty degradations
as now your high-strung
                              martyred resistance serves
to consecrate the liberties of Maastricht?

II

. . . sah er den Erzengel Michael im Kampf gegen den Drachen, Michael, den Engel der deutschen Geschichte . . .

The iron-beamed engine-shed has chapel windows.
Glare-eyed, you spun. The hooks are still in the beam;
a sun-patch drains to nothing; here the chocked
blade sluiced into place, here the abused blood
                   set its own wreaths.
Time passes, strengthening and fading. Europa
hetaera displays her parts, her triumph
to tax even Dürer's resplendent economy
in rictus and graven sorrow.
                     On some envisioned
rathaus clock, geared like a mill, the dragon
strikes,
       the Archangel, unseeing, unbowed,
chimes with each stroke.

Scenes with Harlequins

In Memoriam Aleksandr Blok

Joyfully I accept this strange book, joyfully and with fear — in it there is so much beauty, poetry, death. I await the accomplishment of your task. VOLOKHOVA, TO BLOK, 1907

All the sounds have gone silent. Can't you hear that there aren't any sounds any more? BLOK, in 1920

I

Distance is on edge;
the level tide
stands rimmed with mercury.
Again the estranged spirit

is possessed of light.
The common things
glitter uncommonly.
City besieged by the sun

amid sybilline
galas, a dust
pluming the chariots
of tyrants and invalids,

peppered with mica,
granite-faced seer
scathed by invisible
planets as men dream of war

like a fresh sea-wind
like the lilac
at your petrified heart
as something anciently known . . .

II

The day clacks and birds
gust from the square.
Ferrous sulphate
vapours in the dens

of dead photographers.
With white seraphic
hair against the sun
who are these strangers —

or who are these
charred spirits glaring
their vitreous eyes
towards apocalypse?

They are not of our flesh
to do them justice.
Still they outshine us
among the prophets.

III

Beautiful Lady,
in reverence
with sorrow and masquerade,
how else should we have lived?

Tempestuous fantasies,
blood-tinted opaline
essential clouds,
I am not myself

I think in this last act
without end. Lordly
and faithful servant of Life —
what can one say?

By humour of lament,
spontaneous word of stone,
inspired débâcle
many times rehearsed,

look to abide
tyrannous egality
and freedom led forth
blinded by prophecies.

Now it is gleeting Venus
who so decrees and now
it is parched Mars,
Beautiful Lady.

IV

The risen Christ! Once more
faith is upon us,
a jubilant brief keening
without respite:

Obedience, bitter joy,
the elements, clouds,
winds, louvres where the bell
makes its wild mouths:

Holy Rus — into the rain's
horizons, peacock-dyed
tail-feathers of storm,
so it goes on.

V

Even now one is amazed
by transience: how it
outlasts us all.
Motley of shadow

dabbles the earth,
the malachite bronze
nymphs and sea gods, the pear tree's
motionless wooden leaves.

In this light, constrained spirit,
be a lord of your age.
Rejoice; let the strange
legends begin.

VI

Of Rumor, of Clamor,
I shall be silent;
I will not deal
in the vatic exchanges

between committees,
mysticism by the book.
History is aglow
with bookish fires.

Begone you grave jewellers
and you spartan hoplites
in masks of foil.
Orthodox arcane

interpreters of repute,
this is understood.
Why should I hear
further what you propose?

Exegetes may come
to speak to the silence
that has arisen. It is
not unheard of.

VII

Decembrist blood! We are taxed
for their visions. The earth
turns, returns, through cycles
of declamation;

with feuilletons and iron
fantasies of the state.
Rhadamanthine the grim
torches of naphtha,

the unspeakable dull woe
of which I may have had
foreknowledge — I forget —
in 'Retribution'.

To the Nieuport Scout

How swiftly they cease to be
incredible
       how incredible
the sudden immortals —

a tilt   a flare
as though of mirrors —

dared by their luck
they outdare it
          and spin
from the fumy towers
taking England with them —
flame-tattered
            pirouettes
quenched in a cloud.

Churchill's Funeral

I

. . . one dark day in the Guildhall:
looking at the memorials
of the city's great past &
knowing well the history
of its unending charity,
I seemed to hear far away
in the dim roof a theme,
an echo of some noble melody . . .

Endless London
mourns for that knowledge
under the dim roofs
of smoke-stained glass

the men hefting
their accoutrements
of webbed tin, many
in bandages,

with cigarettes,
with scuffed hands aflare,
as though exhaustion
drew them to life;

as if by some
miraculous draft
of enforced journeys
their peace were made

strange homecoming
into sleep, blighties,
and untouched people
among the maimed:

nobilmente it
rises from silence,
the grand tune, and goes
something like this.

II

Suppose the subject of inquiry,
instead of being House-law (Oikonomia),
had been Star-law (Astronomia),
and that, ignoring distinction
between stars fixed and wandering,
as here between wealth radiant
and wealth reflective, the writer
had begun thus:

Innocent soul
ghosting for its lost
twin, the afflicted one,
born law-giver;

uncanny wraith
kindled afar off
like the evening star,
res publica

seen by itself
with its whole shining
history discerned
through shining air,

both origin
and consequence, its
hierarchies of sorts,
fierce tea-making

in time of war,
courage and kindness
as the marvel is,
the common weal

that will always,
simply as of right,
keep faith, ignorant
of right or fear:

who is to judge
who can judge of this?
Maestros of the world
not you not them.

III

Los listens to the Cry of the Poor Man; his Cloud
Over London in volume terrific low bended in anger.

The copper clouds
are not of this light;
Lambeth is no more
the house of the lamb.

The meek shall die rich
would you believe:
with such poverty
lavished upon them,

with their obsequies
the Heinkels' lourd drone
and Fame darkening
her theatres

to sirens, laughter,
the frizzed angels
of visitation
powdered by the blast,

the catafalques
like gin-palaces
where she entertains
the comedians.

IV

St Mary Abchurch, St Mary Aldermanbury,
St Mary-le-Bow . . .

Stone Pietà
for which the city
offers up incense
and ashes, blitzed

firecrews, martyrs
crying to the Lord,
their mangled voices
within the flame;

to which we bring
litanies of scant
survival and all
random mercies,

with the ragwort
and the willow-herb
as edifiers
of ruined things.

V

. . . every minute particular, the jewels of Albion, running down
The kennels of the streets & lanes as if they were abhorr'd.

The brazed city
reorders its own
destruction, admits
the strutting lords

to the temple,
vandals of sprayed blood
and oblivion
to make their mark.

The spouting head
spiked as prophetic
is ancient news.
Once more the keeper

of the dung-gate
tells his own story;
so too the harlot
of many tears.

Speak now regardless
judges of the hour:
what verdict, what people?
Hem of whose garment?

Whose Jerusalem —
at usance for its bones'
redemption and last
salvo of poppies?

Psalms of Assize

I. Hinc vagantur in tenebris misere,
quia non credunt veritati ipsi . . .
Querunt lumen confisi ipsis et non inveniunt.

Why should I strike you with my name
why trade impress of proud wounds
come now belated
                           patrons of wrath
anxieties are not rectitudes
holiness itself falls
to unholy rejoicing
to resurrect the dead
myth
         of our salvation
blasphemies no less
mercies
            let us pray
Gabriel descend
as a mood almost
                           a monody
of chloroform
or florists roses
consensual angel spinning his words
                           thread
he descends
                  and light
sensitive darkness
                        follows him down

II. Non potest quisquam utrisque servire,
simulque ascendere et descendere;
aut ascendas aut descendas oportet . . .

Ascend through declension
the mass the matter
the gross refinement
    gravitas
everlasting obsession
vanity by grace
the starred
        misattributed
works of survival
attributes even now
hallowing consequence
chants of the trace elements
the Elohim
        unearthly music
given to the world
message what message
        doubtless
the Lord knows
when he will find us
        if ever
we shall see him
with the elect
        justified
to his right hand

Cycle

William Arrowsmith 1924–1992

I

Natural strange beatitudes
                              the leafless tints
of spring touch red through brimstone
what do you mean   praise and lament
it is the willow
                         first then
larch or alder

2

The heart feels for its own
                                      patience
reflects upon itself
light is everywhere
                             the spiders'
galaxies
                  droppings of the
star wormwood

3

So there   there it is   past
reason and measure
                               sustaining
the constancy of mischance
its occlusion
                      a spasm
a psalm

4

Are we not moved by
                    'savage
indignation' or whatever
strange
        natürlich
dance with antlers
paces over and
                over the same
ground

5

· Larch or alder
                first
then willow
            leafless tints
of spring touch red through brimstone

praise and lament
praise and lament

what do you mean
                praise
lament
        praise and lament
what do you mean
                do you mean
beatitudes

Sorrel

Very common and widely distributed . . . It is called
Sorrow . . . in some parts of Worcestershire.

Memory worsening — let it go as rain
streams on half-visible clatter of the wind
                    lapsing and rising,
that clouds the pond's green mistletoe of spawn,
seeps among nettlebeds and rust-brown sorrel,
perpetual ivy burrowed by weak light,
makes carved shapes crumble: the ill-weathering stone
salvation's troth-plight, plumed, of the elect.

NOTES AND
ACKNOWLEDGEMENTS

INDEX

FOR THE UNFALLEN (1959)

The six lines from 'More Sonnets at Christmas, 1942' are quoted from *Collected Poems 1919–1976* by Allen Tate. Copyright © 1977 by Allen Tate. Reprinted by permission of Farrar, Straus & Giroux, Inc.

TENEBRAE (1978)

Spanish and German poems have provided points of departure for several poems in this book. 'The Pentecost Castle' is particularly indebted to J. M. Cohen's *The Penguin Book of Spanish Verse*. The final sonnet of 'Lachrimae' is a free translation of a sonnet by Lope de Vega (Cohen, p. 247) and the second sonnet of 'An Apology . . .' is an imitation of a sonnet by L. L. de Argensola (Cohen, p. 202). The poems by Paul Celan on which I have based my 'Two Chorale-Preludes' are from *Die Niemandsrose* (1963): 'Eis, Eden' and 'Kermorvan'. I have combined a few phrases of free translation with phrases of my own invention.

'A Pre-Raphaelite Notebook' adapts a sentence from Pascal's *Pensées*. The last line of 'Quaint Mazes' is indebted to Ronald Blythe, 'Satan without Seraphs' in the *Listener*, 4 February 1971. 'Te Lucis Ante Terminum' quotes a phrase from Walter J. Ong, S.J., 'Voice as Summons for Belief' (*Literature and Belief: English Institute Essays*, [1957] 1958, p. 84). 'A Short History of British India (I)': see S. P. Carey, *William Carey* (1934 ed.), p. 101.

The epigraphs to 'The Pentecost Castle' are taken from *The Letters of W. B. Yeats,* ed. Allan Wade (London, 1954) and Simone Weil, *First and Last Notebooks,* translated by Richard Rees (Oxford, 1970).

The epigraph to 'Tenebrae' is from Imogen Holst, *The Music of Gustav Holst,* 2nd edition (Oxford, 1968).

THE MYSTERY OF THE CHARITY
OF CHARLES PÉGUY (1984)

2.1: 'poet with the head of a bull': *Poetry,* a tapestry by Jean Lurçat, depicts the twelve signs of the zodiac and a poet with the head of a bull.

2.7: 'Rather the Marne than the *Cahiers*': adapts a phrase from a review-article by P. McCarthy, *TLS,* 16 June 1978, p. 675.

4.1: 'the lords of limit': The phrase is Auden's, from an early poem, 'Now from my window-sill I watch the night'. See Edward Mendelson, ed., *The English Auden* (1977), pp. 115–16.

4.6: 'the camelot-cry of "sticks!"'': *Les camelots du roi* was a right-wing, anti-Dreyfusard organization, prominent in the street battles of the period.

4.6: 'As Tharaud says': Daniel Halévy, *Péguy and 'Les Cahiers de la Quinzaine',* translated from the French by Ruth Bethell (1946), p. 171: 'Always, all through his life, this sound of broken glass, to use Tharaud's expression'.

5.8: 'die for the "terre charnelle"'': Charles Péguy, *Ève* (1913): ' — Heureux ceux qui sont morts pour la terre charnelle, / Mais pourvu que se fût dans une juste guerre.'

7.4: Péguy said ". . . to invoke it"': adapted from Daniel Halévy, *Péguy et 'Les Cahiers de la Quinzaine'* (Paris, 1941: 30° Edition), p. 352.

9.1: 'true tempérament de droite, you have your wish': See Robert Speaight, *Georges Bernanos* (1973), p. 36, for 'what Jacques Maritain has called a *tempérament de droite*'. See also pp. 17–18 for Speaight's view of the great similarities, as well as the great differences, between Bernanos and Péguy.

9.8: '"Je est un autre", that fatal telegram': Arthur Rimbaud, *Lettre à Georges Izambard,* May 1871: 'vous ne comprendrez pas du tout, et je ne saurais presque vous expliquer . . . *Je est un autre* . . .'

10.7: 'Encore plus douloureux et doux': from a quatrain by Charles Péguy.

10.11: 'in memory of those things these words were born': adapts a sentence from Marcel Raymond, *From Baudelaire to Surrealism* (1961), p. 190, referring to Péguy's 'Présentation de la Beauce à Notre-Dame de Chartres'.

NEW POEMS (1992)

'Song Contest'. Anne Hébert's poem 'Les offensés' is to be found in her collection *Le Jour n'a d'Égal que la Nuit*. Copyright © 1992 by Les Éditions du Boréal, Montréal. My imitation appears with the courteous consent of the poet and of her publishers.

'De Jure Belli ac Pacis'. The title is from Grotius. The epigraph for II is from Ger van Roon, *Neuordnung im Widerstand* (München, 1967), p. 155, commenting on a letter of von Haeften, 23 December 1938. A translation of van Roon's book was published in London in 1971 with the title *German Resistance to Hitler: Count von Moltke and the Kreisau Circle;* the corresponding passage can be found there, pp. 54–55.

'Scenes with Harlequins'. The epigraphs are from Avril Pyman, *The Life of Aleksandr Blok,* 2 vols. (Oxford, 1979–80), I, 275; II, 365.

'To the Nieuport Scout'. The Nieuport 17, a French-built fighter introduced in 1916 and flown by a number of early 'aces', British as well as French. Superseded by the Spad S VII.

'Churchill's Funeral'.
   I. The epigraph is from Elgar's note on the original inspiration for his overture *Cockaigne*. It is quoted by Jerrold Northrop Moore, *Edward Elgar: A Creative Life* (Oxford, 1984), p. 342.
   II. The epigraph is from Ruskin, *Unto This Last,* 1862, 'Preface'.
   III. The epigraph is from Blake's *Milton,* 44: 34–35. The 'false' etymology in stanza 1 is true to Blake.
   V. The epigraph is from Blake's *Jerusalem,* 31: 17–18.

'Psalms of Assize'. The Latin quotations are from John Colet's marginalia to the *Epistolae* of Marsilio Ficino. See Sears Jayne, *John Colet and Marsilio Ficino* (Oxford, 1963), pp. 119–20.

'Cycle'. I take 'savage indignation' from Yeats's 'Swift's Epitaph', which translates Swift's own Latin ('*saeva indignatio*').

'Sorrel'. 'Very common and widely distributed . . .': I have taken this description from John Amphlett and Carleton Rea, *The Botany of Worcestershire* (Birmingham, 1909), p. 317.

Several of the new poems have previously appeared in print, in the United Kingdom, in *Agenda*, the *Sunday Correspondent*, the *Times*, and the *Times Literary Supplement*.

INDEX OF TITLES AND FIRST LINES

A lost storm in this temperate
place, 75
A pet-name, a common name.
Best-selling brand, curt
(Mercian Hymns, II), 94
A way of many ways: a god,
41
A workable fancy. Old
petulant, 83
Abrupt tempter; close enough
to survive, 33
After Cumae, 32
Against the burly air I strode,
3
among the beetroots, where
we are constrained, 170
And, after all, it is to them we
return, 140
And it seemed, while we
waited, he began to walk
towards us   he vanished
(Mercian Hymns, XXX),
122
And now the sea-scoured
temptress, having failed,
23
And you my spent heart's
treasure, 129
And you, who with your soft
but searching voice, 160
Angel of Tones, 187
Anguish bloated by the replete
scream, 78
Annunciations, 50–51
Anything to have done, 14
*Apology, for the Revival of
Christian Architecture in
England, An*, 140–152

Apostles, The, 35
As he is wounded, 132
As with torches we go, at wild
Christmas, 62
Ascend through declension,
210
Asmodeus, 16–17
Assisi Fragments, The, 71
At dawn the Mass, 127
At Pavia, a visitation of some
sorrow. Boethius'
(Mercian Hymns, XVIII),
110
Autumn resumes the land,
ruffles the woods, 148
Ave Regina Coelorum, 153

Beautiful Lady, 196
Behind the thorn-trees thin
smoke, scutch-grass or
(Mercian Hymns, XIX),
111
Below, the river scrambled
like a goat, 6
Bibliographers, The, 34
Bidden Guest, The, 9–10
Bonhoeffer in his skylit cell,
159
Briefly they are amazed.
The marigold-fields,
156
Brooding on the eightieth
letter of *Fors Clavigera*
(Mercian Hymns, XXV),
117
By order of hunger the
starving stood in line,
191

Canaan, 188–189
Canticle for Good Friday, 27
Centaury with your staunch
    bloom, 154
'Christmas Trees,' 159
Churchill's Funeral, 202–208
Clash of salutation. As keels
    thrust into shingle
    (Mercian Hymns, XVI),
    108
Cohorts of charabancs
    fanfared Offa's province
    and (Mercian Hymns,
    XXI), 113
Coins handsome as Nero's; of
    good substance and
    (Mercian Hymns, XI), 103
Coplas, 81
Cowan Bridge: At the site of
    'Lowood School,' 75
Crack of a starting-pistol. Jean
    Jaurès, 165
Created purely from glass the
    saint stands, 45
Crucified Lord, however
    much I burn, 136
Crucified Lord, so naked to
    the world, 138
Crucified Lord, you swim
    upon your cross, 133
Cycle: William Arrowsmith
    1924–1992, 211–213

Damon's Lament for his
    Clorinda, Yorkshire 1654,
    141
Darkness, 67
Dawnlight freezes against the
    east-wire, 54
Dead Bride, The, 79
Death of Shelley, The, 37
De Jure Belli ac Pacis, 192–193

Dear lords of life, stump-
    toothed, with ragged
    breath, 175
Decembrist blood! We are
    taxed, 200
Difficult friend, I would have
    preferred, 69
Dismissing reports and men,
    he put pressure on the
    (Mercian Hymns, XIV),
    106
Distance is on edge, 194
Distant Fury of Battle, The,
    15
Do words make up the
    majesty, 77
Doctor Faustus, 41–42
Domaine Public, 68
Doubtless he saw some path
    clear, having found, 25
Down in the orchard, 126
Down in the river-garden a
    grey-gold, 177
Drake's Drum, 24
Dry walls, and nettles battered
    by the dust, 76

Each day the tide withdraws;
    chills us; pastes, 30
Eia ergo. For this is Sion's
    twin city, 181
Eia, with handbells, jews'
    harps, risible, 180
Elegiac Stanzas: On a Visit to
    Dove Cottage, 31
Endless London, 202
Europe, the much-scarred,
    much-scoured terrain, 36
Evasive souls, of whom the
    wise lose track, 70
Eve of St Mark, The, 151
Even now one is amazed, 198

Fantasia on 'Horbury': John Bacchus Dykes, 1859, 76
Fear, The, 21
Fidelities, 149
Florentines, 158
For all that must be gone through, their long death, 20
For reading I can recommend, 68
For whom do we scrape our tribute of pain, 59
For whom the possessed sea littered, on both shores, 18
Fortified in their front parlours, at Yuletide men *(Mercian Hymns, XXVI)* 118
Four Poems Regarding the Endurance of Poets, 66–69
From the Latin, 86
Funeral Music, 58–65

Gasholders, russet among fields. Milldams, marlpools *(Mercian Hymns, VII)*, 99
Genesis, 3–5
God's Little Mountain, 6
Goldfinch and hawk, 127
Grass resurrects to mask, to strangle, 15
Guardians, The, 28

Having stood hungrily apart, 41
He adored the desk, its brown-oak inlaid with ebony *(Mercian Hymns, X)*, 102

He drove at evening through the hushed Vosges. The *(Mercian Hymns, XVII)*, 109
He was the surveyor of his own ice-world, 56
He wounds with ecstasy. All, 162
Herefordshire Carol, The, 152
High voices in domestic chapels; praise, 142
History as Poetry, 72
Holy Thursday, 7
Horses, black-lidded mouths peeled back, 158
How swiftly they cease to be, 201
Humanist, The, 57
Hymns to Our Lady of Chartres, 180–182

I Had Hope When Violence Was Ceas't, 54
I imagine, as I imagine us, 85
I love my work and my children. God, 49
I shall go down, 132
I was invested in mother-earth, the crypt of roots *(Mercian Hymns, IV)*, 96
I went out early, 128
I will consider the outnumbering dead, 8
Idylls of the King, 150
If the night is dark, 130
Imaginative Life, The, 70
In Memory of Jane Fraser, 11
In Piam Memoriam, 45
In tapestries, in dreams, they gathered, as it was enacted *(Mercian Hymns, XXIII)*, 115

Iniquity passes, 189
Innocent soul, 204
Itinerant through numerous
   domains, of his lord's
   (Mercian Hymns, XXIV),
   116

King of the perennial holly-
   groves, the riven
   sandstone *(Mercian
   Hymns, I),* 93
Knowing the dead, and how
   some are disposed, 19

*Lachrimae: or Seven tears figured
   in seven passionate Pavans,*
   133–139
Lachrimae Amantis, 139
Lachrimae Antiquae Novae, 138
Lachrimae Coactae, 136
Laurel Axe, The, 148
Let mind be more precious
   than soul; it will not, 61
Letter from Armenia, A, 87
Lion and lioness, the mild, 71
*Little Apocalypse: Hölderlin:
   1770–1843,* 33
Locust Songs, 52–53
Loss and Gain, 146
Love, oh my love, it will
   come, 84
Love that drained her drained
   him she'd loved, though
   each, 12
Loves I allow and passions I
   approve, 137
Lowlands of Holland, The, 36
Lucifer blazing in superb
   effigies, 34

Make miniatures of the once-
   monstrous theme, 143

Malcolm and Frere,
   Colebrooke and
   Elphinstone, 145
Married and not for love, 131
Martyrdom of St Sebastian, The,
   40
Martyrium, 135
Masque of Blackness, The, 134
Memory worsening — let it
   go as rain, 213
Men Are a Mockery of Angels, 66
Mercian Hymns, 91–122
Merlin, 8
Metamorphoses, 21–25
Mobile, immaculate and
   austere, 43
Mountains, monuments, all
   forms, 31
Music survives, composing
   her own sphere, 162
My little son, when you could
   command marvels, 63
*Mystery of the Charity of
   Charles Péguy, The,* 163–
   179

Naked, as if for swimming,
   the martyr, 40
Naked, he climbed to the
   wolf's lair, 7
Natural strange beatitudes,
   211
No manner of address will do,
   21
Not as we are but as we must
   appear, 65
'Not strangeness, but strange
   likeness. Obstinate'
   (Mercian Hymns, XXIX),
   121
November rips gold foil from
   the oak ridges, 141

'Now when King Offa was alive and dead,' they were *(Mercian Hymns, XXVII)*, 119

O light of light, supreme delight, 161
O Love, subject of the mere diurnal grind, 51
O stamping-ground of the shod Word! So hard, 53
Ode on the Loss of the 'Titanic,' 39
Of Coming-into-Being and Passing-Away, 186
Of Commerce and Society: Variations on a Theme, 35–40
Of Rumor, of Clamor, 199
Old Poet with Distant Admirers, 74
On the morning of the crowning we chorused our *(Mercian Hymns, III)*, 95
'One cannot lose what one has not possessed,' 81
Order of Service, An, 56
Orpheus and Eurydice, 44
Out of the foliage of sensual pride, 52
Ovid in the Third Reich, 49

Pastoral, A, 43
Pavana Dolorosa, 137
Pentecost Castle, The, 125–132
Picture of a Nativity, 26
Pitched high above the shallows of the sea, 146
Poetry as salutation; taste, 72
Postures, 85
Prayer to the Sun, A, 67

Pre-Raphaelite Notebook, A, 155
Primeval heathland spattered with the bones of mice *(Mercian Hymns, XX)*, 112
Primroses; salutations; the miry skull, 155
Processes of generation; deeds of settlement. The *(Mercian Hymns, XXVIII)*, 120
Processionals in the exemplary cave, 58
Prodigal of loves and barbecues, 46
'Prowess, vanity, mutual regard, 64
Psalms of Assize, 209–210

Quaint Mazes, 140

Rage and regret are tireless to explain, 166
Re-birth of Venus, The, 23
Recall, now, the omens of childhood, 73
Redemptrice of all vows and fealties, Dame, 182
Remember how, at seven years, the decrees, 149
Requiem for the Plantagenet Kings, 18
Requite this angel whose, 160
Respublica, 190
Ritornelli, 187
Rosa sericea: its red, 186
Roughly-silvered leaves that are the snow, 88

St James and St John, 130
Salute us all, Christus with your iron, 174

Scarcely speaking: it becomes
    as a, 90
Scenes with Harlequins, 194–
    200
Sea-preserved, heaped with
    sea-spoils, 26
September Song, 55
Short History of British India,
    A, 143–145
Slime; the residues of refined
    tears, 37
Slowly my heron flies, 128
So much for the elves'
    wergild, the true
    governance (Mercian
    Hymns, V), 97
So much he had from fashion
    and no more, 13
So, remotely, in your part of
    the world, 87
So to celebrate that kingdom:
    it grows, 152
So white I was, he would have
    me cry, 79
So with sweet oaths
    converting the salt earth,
    52
Sobieski's Shield, 185
Soliloquies, 73–74
Solomon's Mines, 14
Some days a shadow through,
    66
Song Contest, 191
Song from Armenia, A, 88
Songbook of Sebastian Arrurruz,
    The: Sebastian Arrurruz:
    1868–1922, 80–90
Sorrel, 213
Splendidly-shining darkness,
    131
Splendour of life so splendidly
    contained, 134

Statesmen have known
    visions. And, not alone,
    38
Stone Man, The, 73
Stone Pietà, 207
Stroke the small silk with your
    whispering hands, 151
Stupefying images of grief-in-
    dream, 161
Suppose they sweltered here
    three thousand years,
    144

Te Lucis Ante Terminum, 154
Ten years without you. For so
    it happens, 80
Tenebrae, 160–162
Terribilis est Locus Iste: Gauguin
    and the Pont-Aven School,
    156
The blackberry, white, 185
The brazed city, 208
The copper clouds, 206
The crocus armies from the
    dead, 157
The cross staggered him. At
    the cliff-top, 27
The day clacks and birds, 195
The Innocents have not flown,
    42
The iron-beamed engine-shed
    has chapel windows, 193
The Jesus-faced man walking
    crowned with flies, 135
The mad are predators. Too
    often lately they harbour
    (Mercian Hymns, VIII),
    100
The night, then; bravely
    stiffen; you are one, 17
The people moves as one spirit
    unfettered, 192

The pigeon purrs in the wood;
the wood has gone, 150
The princes of Mercia were
badger and raven. Thrall
(Mercian Hymns, VI), 98
The risen Christ! Once more,
197
The starched unbending
candles stir, 9
The strange church smelled a
bit 'high,' of censers
(Mercian Hymns, IX), 101
The strident high, 190
The sun again unearthed,
colours come up fresh, 32
The *Venice* portrait: he, 57
The Word has been abroad, is
back, with a tanned look,
50
The young, having risen early,
had gone, 28
Their spades grafted through
the variably-resistant
(Mercian Hymns, XII),
104
There is a land called Lost, 153
There is an ancient landscape
of green branches, 176
There would have been things
to say, quietness, 86
They, after the slow building
of the house, 16
They bespoke doomsday and
they meant it by, 60
They march at God's, 188
They sat. They stood about,
35
They slew by night, 125
This is the ash-pit of the lily-
fire, 162
This love will see me dead,
129

This world is different,
belongs to them, 168
Those varied dead. The
undiscerning sea, 24
Though there are wild dogs,
44
Three Baroque Meditations, 77–
79
Thriving against façades the
ignorant sea, 39
Through scant pride to be so
put out, 22
To dispense, with justice; or,
to dispense, 172
To His Wife, 89
To the Nieuport Scout, 201
To the (Supposed) Patron, 46
Trim the lamp; polish the lens;
draw, one by one, rare
(Mercian Hymns, XIII),
105
Tristia: 1891–1938, 69
Troublesome Reign, The, 11
Turtle Dove, The, 12
Tutting, he wrenched at a
snarled root of dead
crab-apple *(Mercian
Hymns, XV)*, 107
*Two Chorale-Preludes: on
melodies by Paul Celan*,
153–154
Two Formal Elegies, 19–20

Undesirable you may have
been, untouchable, 55

Veni Coronaberis, 157
Veni Redemptor, but not in
our time, 161
Vistas of richness and reward.
The cedar, 167
Vocations, 197

We ran across the meadow
  scabbed with cow-dung,
  past *(Mercian Hymns,
  XXII)*, 114
What I lost was not a part of
  this, 74
What is there in my heart
  that you should sue,
  139
What other men do with other
  women, 82
When snow like sheep lay in
  the fold, 11

Where the living with effort
  go, 29
While friends defected, you
  stayed and were sure, 147
White Ship, The, 29
*Who Are These Coming to the
  Sacrifice?*, 142
Why should I strike you with
  my name, 209
Wreaths, 30

You ventured occasionally, 89
You watchers on the wall, 126